DATA
COMMUNICATIONS
AND LOCAL AREA
NETWORKING
HANDBOOK

BRITT RORABAUGH

TAB Professional and Reference Books

Division of TAB BOOKS Inc.
P.O. Box 40, Blue Ridge Summit, PA 17214

TOUCHTONE is a registered trademark of American Telephone and Telegraph Co.

FIRST EDITION
FIRST PRINTING

Copyright © 1985 by TAB BOOKS Inc.
Printed in the United States of America

Library of Congress Cataloging in Publication Data

Rorabaugh, Britt.
Data communications and local area networking
handbook.

Includes index.
1. Data transmission systems.   2. Local area
networks (Computer networks)   I. Title.
TK5105.R65   1985   004.6   85-22186
ISBN 0-8306-0603-3

Contents

Introduction

THIS BOOK IS AN EASY TO UNDERSTAND INTRODUCTION TO THE THEORY AND practices of data communications and local area networking. It will prove useful to virtually anyone concerned with the theory or practice of data communications—students, hobbyists, programmers, engineers, and managers or buyers of office automation equipment and systems.

Rather than concentrate on a few specific topics as many books in this area have done, this book intentionally presents a "broad-brush" introduction to many issues that pertain to successful data communications. The earlier chapters concern fundamental techniques and an exploration of the traditional "remote terminal to distant host" type of communications. The later chapters contain discussions of modern data communications techniques as applied to local area networking. This approach will prepare both technically and nontechnically oriented users of computer systems to intelligently select and employ the appropriate data communications measures for a variety of applications.

To Joyce, Geoff, and Amber

Chapter 1

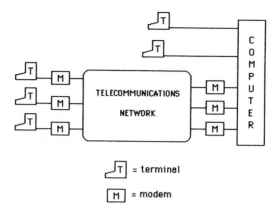

_T_ = terminal

[M] = modem

Introduction to
Data Communications

E ARLY DATA COMMUNICATIONS WERE RELATIVELY SIMPLE—BEGINNING WITH
telegraphy and then evolving to include teletype circuits and simple remote
terminal connections to host mainframe computers. Today data communications is
far from simple with numerous standards, protocols, software, and hardware to choose
from. In this chapter we will examine the OSI model, which was developed to bring
some order and structure to this chaotic situation, and we will see how some of the
practices and standards developed for classical applications fit into this relatively
new generalized framework.

REMOTE TERMINALS

Figure 1-1 shows a hypothetical computer with a number of terminals connected
to it. In data communications terminology the computer and terminals are referred
to as *Data Terminal Equipment* or *DTE*. Some terminals are connected directly to
the computer, but in most cases truly remote terminals will be connected to the computer via a public telecommunications network and a pair of modems. Modems and
similar equipment are called *Data Circuit-Terminating Equipment, Data Communications Equipment,* or *DCE* in data communications standards, while they are called
datasets in Bell System literature. In a book on data communications written a few
years ago remote terminal interfacing might be the only application of interest, but
it is now beginning to be dwarfed by the explosion in distributed systems and local
networking applications.

ISO OPEN SYSTEMS INTERCONNECT

In an effort to establish a common reference for ongoing and future efforts, the In-

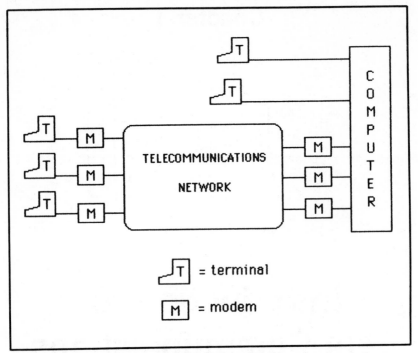

Fig. 1-1. Remote terminals connected to host computer.

ternational Standards Organization (ISO) has drafted a generalized model of the complete data communications process. This model is called the *Open Systems Interconnect (OSI)* model and is divided into seven layers as shown in Fig. 1-2. The model was designed to be very complete and cover a wide variety of situations, and as a consequence there is a great deal of detail in the model that either doesn't apply in all situations or which is sometimes difficult to correlate with the actual structure of many working communications systems. Maybe the structure of future systems will agree with the OSI model, but right now most systems only partially adhere to the model with most of the emphasis on standards for the physical, data-link control, and network layers. These layers are generally hardware dependent and although many standards for them exist, the particular standards selected and their implementation will vary greatly from installation to installation. The session, presentation, and applications layers are more software dependent and tend to be unique to each particular application. However, the intent is for these layers to be standardized to facilitate intercommunication between diverse machines. Work goes on to establish standards for these upper layers, but it will be a while before anything useful emerges. The transport layer will act as an interface between the installation-specific lower layers and the standardized upper layers.

Physical Layer

Layer 1 or the physical layer of an interconnection defines the physical link between two communicating devices. Generally this definition comprises four principal characteristics—mechanical, electrical, functional, and procedural. Connector specifications and the allocation of connector pins are the primary mechanical concerns, while electrical concerns include: output impedances of signal generators, in-

2

put impedances of signal receivers, voltage and current levels, and pulse transistion times. Functional characteristics deal with the specific purpose of each circuit in the interface, while the procedural aspects deal with the usage of the interface circuits to accomplish various tasks in the bit transmission process.

As shown in Fig. 1-3, the physical layer can appear at a number of different locations depending on the system configuration. In remote terminal applications, the physical layer of the DTE-to-DCE interface is addressed by EIA standards RS-232-C, RS-449, RS-422-A, and RS-423-A, which are discussed in Chapter 7. In cases where the DCE is a modem, the physical interface between the DCE and the transmission facility is defined in the applicable modem standard. Bell System 103, 202, and 212 modem standards are discussed in Chapter 8. Even though not intended for such use, existing physical layer specifications can be modified to define DTE-to-DTE interfaces. In the small computer arena, elements of RS-232-C are widely used to interface a variety of computers and peripherals. Work is underway to formally define new standards for such applications, but meanwhile ad hoc adaptation of RS-232-C and RS-449 continues to fill the void.

Data-Link Control Layer

Layer 2 or the data-link control layer deals with the logical aspects of transmitting data over the physical links defined by layer 1. When two stations are to begin com-

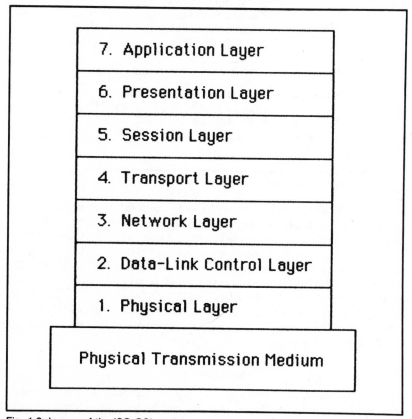

Fig. 1-2. Layers of the ISO OSI model.

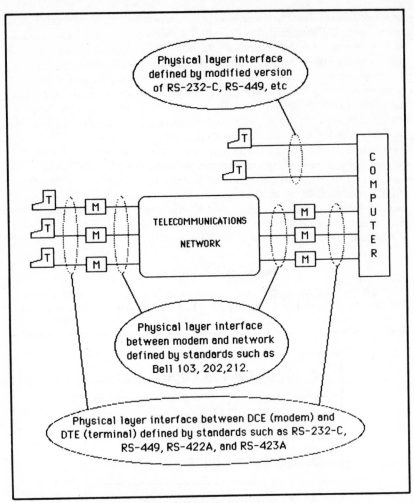

Fig. 1-3. Physical layer interface standards.

municating, the datalink control protocol must first establish an active link between them. Once communications are established, the protocol must maintain control of byte synchronization, datablock framing, error detection and correction, and rate of data flow on the link. Protocols for the datalink control layer can take three basic forms—character-oriented, bit oriented, or multiaccess. *IBM Bisync, ANSI X3.28*, and virtually all hobbyist protocols are examples of *character-oriented protocols*, which are discussed in Chapter 11. *ISO HDLC* and *IBM SDLC*, discussed in Chapter 12, are examples of *bit-oriented protocols*. Multiaccess schemes are discussed in general terms in Chapter 13, while the most commonly encountered example, *Ethernet*, is explained in Chapter 14.

Network Layer

The network layer is concerned with the routing of data from the source terminal to the destination terminal. This is a major issue in the design of local area networks and large computer networks. In the traditional "remote terminal to single host" type of communications, however, routing concerns are relatively transparent to the designer of a single remote terminal installation.

Transport Layer

The major purpose of the transport layer is to act as an interface between the relatively hardware-oriented lower layers and the software-oriented upper layers, relieving these layers from any concern over the actual mechanics of the actual communications process.

Session Layer

The session layer provides file management and "bookkeeping" functions needed to support intersystem communications.

Presentation Layer

The presentation layer provides the necessary services to interface a wide variety of applications to the communications system without requiring modifications to or special design of the applications software. It is in this layer that data compression, format conversion, and encryption usually take place.

Application Layer

The application layer is that portion of an application that is concerned with the interface to the presentation layer for the purpose of conducting data communication. This layer is almost completely application and user dependent.

SUMMARY

The physical and data-link control layers address classical data communications issues such as physical and electrical characteristics of the transmitted signals, data coding, synchronization of data signals, and error detection and correction, which are all covered in this book. Also covered are elements of local area networking such as network topology, routing, and access control schemes that are addressed in the data-link control and network layers. The remaining layers of the ISO OSI model deal with software issues that are presently highly machine dependent and, except for data compression and encryption, beyond the scope of this book.

Chapter 2

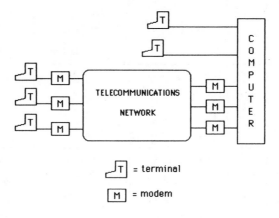

$\boxed{\text{T}}$ = terminal

$\boxed{\text{M}}$ = modem

Data Coding

M OST DIGITAL DATA IS TRANSMITTED IN EITHER NUMERIC OR TEXT FORM. Numeric data can be represented in integer, fixed point, or floating point formats, and text data can be encoded using a number of different *data codes*. By far, the greatest volume of data is transmitted as text, with numeric data being "spelled out" as text, digit by digit. Data codes should not be confused with *line codes*, which will be discussed in Chapter 4. Digital information always makes use of some numeric format or data code in which the data of interest are represented as a sequence of binary bits. These bits may then be encoded using a line code to yield a sequence of signal levels suitable for long-distance transmission. In this chapter we will examine some of the more common data codes and error detection schemes. Then we will move on to some data compression coding techniques which allow transmission of more data in fewer bits than is possible when using a "standard" data code such as ASCII. Finally we will finish up with a look at some data encryption techniques which can provide some security and privacy when sensitive data is to be sent over public networks.

BAUDOT CODES

In asynchronous communications, if the clock rates differ greatly between the transmitting device and the receiving device, the sampling of the last few bits in each character can be performed incorrectly. That's why in the early days of electromechanical teleprinter communications, the character codes were generally limited to five bits per character. Tables 2-1 through 2-6 show some variations on a five bit code which is often incorrectly referred to as the *Baudot* code. None of these variations (which are actually based on a five bit code developed for telegraphy by Donald Murray) resembles either of the five bit codes shown in Tables 2-7 and 2-8,

Table 2-1. CCITT Alphabet #2.

Dec	Hex	Oct	Binary	Letters Mode Character	Figures Mode Character
00	00	00	0 0 0 0 0	blank	blank
01	01	01	0 0 0 0 1	E	3
02	02	02	0 0 0 1 0	LF	LF
03	03	03	0 0 0 1 1	A	-
04	04	04	0 0 1 0 0	space	space
05	05	05	0 0 1 0 1	S	' (apos)
06	06	06	0 0 1 1 0	I	8
07	07	07	0 0 1 1 1	U	7
08	08	10	0 1 0 0 0	CR	CR
09	09	11	0 1 0 0 1	D	WRU
10	0A	12	0 1 0 1 0	R	4
11	0B	13	0 1 0 1 1	J	BELL
12	0C	14	0 1 1 0 0	N	, (comma)
13	0D	15	0 1 1 0 1	F	
14	0E	16	0 1 1 1 0	C	:
15	0F	17	0 1 1 1 1	K	(
16	10	20	1 0 0 0 0	T	5
17	11	21	1 0 0 0 1	Z	+
18	12	22	1 0 0 1 0	L	)
19	13	23	1 0 0 1 1	W	2
20	14	24	1 0 1 0 0	H	
21	15	25	1 0 1 0 1	Y	6
22	16	26	1 0 1 1 0	P	0
23	17	27	1 0 1 1 1	Q	1
24	18	30	1 1 0 0 0	O	9
25	19	31	1 1 0 0 1	B	?
26	1A	32	1 1 0 1 0	G	
27	1B	33	1 1 0 1 1	FIGS	FIGS
28	1C	34	1 1 1 0 0	M	. (period)
29	1D	35	1 1 1 0 1	X	/
30	1E	36	1 1 1 1 0	V	=
31	1F	37	1 1 1 1 1	LTRS	LTRS

Table 2-2. Western Union "A" Keyboard Five Bit Code.

Dec	Hex	Oct	Binary	Letters Mode Character	Figures Mode Character
00	00	00	0 0 0 0 0	blank	blank
01	01	01	0 0 0 0 1	E	3
02	02	02	0 0 0 1 0	LF	LF
03	03	03	0 0 0 1 1	A	-
04	04	04	0 0 1 0 0	space	space
05	05	05	0 0 1 0 1	S	' (apos)
06	06	06	0 0 1 1 0	I	8
07	07	07	0 0 1 1 1	U	7
08	08	10	0 1 0 0 0	CR	CR
09	09	11	0 1 0 0 1	D	$
10	0A	12	0 1 0 1 0	R	4
11	0B	13	0 1 0 1 1	J	BELL
12	0C	14	0 1 1 0 0	N	, (comma)
13	0D	15	0 1 1 0 1	F	
14	0E	16	0 1 1 1 0	C	:
15	0F	17	0 1 1 1 1	K	(
16	10	20	1 0 0 0 0	T	5
17	·11	21	1 0 0 0 1	Z	"
18	12	22	1 0 0 1 0	L	)
19	13	23	1 0 0 1 1	W	2
20	14	24	1 0 1 0 0	H	#
21	15	25	1 0 1 0 1	Y	6
22	16	26	1 0 1 1 0	P	0
23	17	27	1 0 1 1 1	Q	1
24	18	30	1 1 0 0 0	O	9
25	19	31	1 1 0 0 1	B	?
26	1A	32	1 1 0 1 0	G	&
27	1B	33	1 1 0 1 1	FIGS	FIGS
28	1C	34	1 1 1 0 0	M	. (period)
29	1D	35	1 1 1 0 1	X	/
30	1E	36	1 1 1 1 0	V	;
31	1F	37	1 1 1 1 1	LTRS	LTRS

Table 2-3. Western Union TELEX Five Bit Code.

Dec	Hex	Oct	Binary	Letters Mode Character	Figures Mode Character
00	00	00	0 0 0 0 0	blank	blank
01	01	01	0 0 0 0 1	E	3
02	02	02	0 0 0 1 0	LF	LF
03	03	03	0 0 0 1 1	A	-
04	04	04	0 0 1 0 0	space	space
05	05	05	0 0 1 0 1	S	' (apos)
06	06	06	0 0 1 1 0	I	8
07	07	07	0 0 1 1 1	U	7
08	08	10	0 1 0 0 0	CR	CR
09	09	11	0 1 0 0 1	D	WRU
10	0A	12	0 1 0 1 0	R	4
11	0B	13	0 1 0 1 1	J	BELL
12	0C	14	0 1 1 0 0	N	, (comma)
13	0D	15	0 1 1 0 1	F	$
14	0E	16	0 1 1 1 0	C	:
15	0F	17	0 1 1 1 1	K	(
16	10	20	1 0 0 0 0	T	5
17	·11	21	1 0 0 0 1	Z	"
18	12	22	1 0 0 1 0	L	)
19	13	23	1 0 0 1 1	W	2
20	14	24	1 0 1 0 0	H	#
21	15	25	1 0 1 0 1	Y	6
22	16	26	1 0 1 1 0	P	0
23	17	27	1 0 1 1 1	Q	1
24	18	30	1 1 0 0 0	O	9
25	19	31	1 1 0 0 1	B	?
26	1A	32	1 1 0 1 0	G	&
27	1B	33	1 1 0 1 1	FIGS	FIGS
28	1C	34	1 1 1 0 0	M	. (period)
29	1D	35	1 1 1 0 1	X	/
30	1E	36	1 1 1 1 0	V	;
31	1F	37	1 1 1 1 1	LTRS	LTRS

Table 2-4. Western Union Telegraph Five Bit Code.

Dec	Hex	Oct	Binary	Letters Mode Character	Figures Mode Character
00	00	00	0 0 0 0 0	blank	blank
01	01	01	0 0 0 0 1	E	3
02	02	02	0 0 0 1 0	LF	LF
03	03	03	0 0 0 1 1	A	-
04	04	04	0 0 1 0 0	space	space
05	05	05	0 0 1 0 1	S	THRU
06	06	06	0 0 1 1 0	I	8
07	07	07	0 0 1 1 1	U	7
08	08	10	0 1 0 0 0	CR	CR
09	09	11	0 1 0 0 1	D	$
10	0A	12	0 1 0 1 0	R	4
11	0B	13	0 1 0 1 1	J	BELL
12	0C	14	0 1 1 0 0	N	, (comma)
13	0D	15	0 1 1 0 1	F	CITY
14	0E	16	0 1 1 1 0	C	:
15	0F	17	0 1 1 1 1	K	(
16	10	20	1 0 0 0 0	T	5
17	·11	21	1 0 0 0 1	Z	"
18	12	22	1 0 0 1 0	L	)
19	13	23	1 0 0 1 1	W	2
20	14	24	1 0 1 0 0	H	£
21	15	25	1 0 1 0 1	Y	6
22	16	26	1 0 1 1 0	P	0
23	17	27	1 0 1 1 1	Q	1
24	18	30	1 1 0 0 0	O	9
25	19	31	1 1 0 0 1	B	?
26	1A	32	1 1 0 1 0	G	&
27	1B	33	1 1 0 1 1	FIGS	FIGS
28	1C	34	1 1 1 0 0	M	. (period)
29	1D	35	1 1 1 0 1	X	/
30	1E	36	1 1 1 1 0	V	;
31	1F	37	1 1 1 1 1	LTRS	LTRS

Table 2-5. United Press International Five Bit Code.

Dec	Hex	Oct	Binary	Letters Mode Character	Figures Mode Character
00	00	00	0 0 0 0 0	blank	blank
01	01	01	0 0 0 0 1	E	3
02	02	02	0 0 0 1 0	LF	LF
03	03	03	0 0 0 1 1	A	-
04	04	04	0 0 1 0 0	space	space
05	05	05	0 0 1 0 1	S	BELL
06	06	06	0 0 1 1 0	I	8
07	07	07	0 0 1 1 1	U	7
08	08	10	0 1 0 0 0	CR	CR
09	09	11	0 1 0 0 1	D	$
10	0A	12	0 1 0 1 0	R	4
11	0B	13	0 1 0 1 1	J	' (apos)
12	0C	14	0 1 1 0 0	N	, (comma)
13	0D	15	0 1 1 0 1	F	!
14	0E	16	0 1 1 1 0	C	:
15	0F	17	0 1 1 1 1	K	(
16	10	20	1 0 0 0 0	T	5
17	·11	21	1 0 0 0 1	Z	"
18	12	22	1 0 0 1 0	L	)
19	13	23	1 0 0 1 1	W	2
20	14	24	1 0 1 0 0	H	£
21	15	25	1 0 1 0 1	Y	6
22	16	26	1 0 1 1 0	P	0
23	17	27	1 0 1 1 1	Q	1
24	18	30	1 1 0 0 0	O	9
25	19	31	1 1 0 0 1	B	?
26	1A	32	1 1 0 1 0	G	&
27	1B	33	1 1 0 1 1	FIGS	FIGS
28	1C	34	1 1 1 0 0	M	. (period)
29	1D	35	1 1 1 0 1	X	/
30	1E	36	1 1 1 1 0	V	;
31	1F	37	1 1 1 1 1	LTRS	LTRS

Table 2-6. Elliot 803 Telecode.

Dec	Hex	Oct	Binary	Letters Mode Character	Figures Mode Character
00	00	00	0 0 0 0 0	blank	blank
01	01	01	0 0 0 0 1	A	1
02	02	02	0 0 0 1 0	B	2
03	03	03	0 0 0 1 1	C	8
04	04	04	0 0 1 0 0	D	4
05	05	05	0 0 1 0 1	E	&
06	06	06	0 0 1 1 0	F	=
07	07	07	0 0 1 1 1	G	7
08	08	10	0 1 0 0 0	H	8
09	09	11	0 1 0 0 1	I	' (apos)
10	0A	12	0 1 0 1 0	J	, (comma)
11	0B	13	0 1 0 1 1	K	+
12	0C	14	0 1 1 0 0	L	:
13	0D	15	0 1 1 0 1	M	-
14	0E	16	0 1 1 1 0	N	. (period)
15	0F	17	0 1 1 1 1	O	%
16	10	20	1 0 0 0 0	P	0
17	11	21	1 0 0 0 1	Q	(
18	12	22	1 0 0 1 0	R	)
19	13	23	1 0 0 1 1	S	3
20	14	24	1 0 1 0 0	T	?
21	15	25	1 0 1 0 1	U	5
22	16	26	1 0 1 1 0	V	6
23	17	27	1 0 1 1 1	W	/
24	18	30	1 1 0 0 0	X	@
25	19	31	1 1 0 0 1	Y	9
26	1A	32	1 1 0 1 0	Z	£
27	1B	33	1 1 0 1 1	FIGS	FIGS
28	1C	34	1 1 1 0 0	space	space
29	1D	35	1 1 1 0 1	return	return
30	1E	36	1 1 1 1 0	LF	LF
31	1F	37	1 1 1 1 1	LTRS	LTRS

**Table 2-7. True Baudot Code Used in
Continental Service by the British Post Office, 1897-1935.**

Dec	Hex	Oct	Binary	Letters Mode Character	Figures Mode Character
00	00	00	0 0 0 0 0	blank	blank
01	01	01	0 0 0 0 1	A	1
02	02	02	0 0 0 1 0	E	2
03	03	03	0 0 0 1 1	E'	&
04	04	04	0 0 1 0 0	Y	3
05	05	05	0 0 1 0 1	U	4
06	06	06	0 0 1 1 0	I	$\underline{o}$
07	07	07	0 0 1 1 1	O	5
08	08	10	0 1 0 0 0	fig blank	fig blank
09	09	11	0 1 0 0 1	J	6
10	0A	12	0 1 0 1 0	G	7
11	0B	13	0 1 0 1 1	H	$\underline{\underline{H}}$
12	0C	14	0 1 1 0 0	B	8
13	0D	15	0 1 1 0 1	C	9
14	0E	16	0 1 1 1 0	F	$\underline{F}$
15	0F	17	0 1 1 1 1	D	Ø
16	10	20	1 0 0 0 0	letr blnk	letr blnk
17	11	21	1 0 0 0 1	$\underline{\underline{t}}$	.
18	12	22	1 0 0 1 0	X	,
19	13	23	1 0 0 1 1	Z	:
20	14	24	1 0 1 0 0	S	;
21	15	25	1 0 1 0 1	T	!
22	16	26	1 0 1 1 0	W	?
23	17	27	1 0 1 1 1	V	'
24	18	30	1 1 0 0 0	erasure	erasure
25	19	31	1 1 0 0 1	K	(
26	1A	32	1 1 0 1 0	M	)
27	1B	33	1 1 0 1 1	L	=
28	1C	34	1 1 1 0 0	R	-
29	1D	35	1 1 1 0 1	Q	/
30	1E	36	1 1 1 1 0	N	Nọ
31	1F	37	1 1 1 1 1	P	%

Table 2-8. True Baudot Code Used in Inland Service by the British Post Office, 1897-1935.

Dec	Hex	Oct	Binary	Letters Mode Character	Figures Mode Character
00	00	00	0 0 0 0 0	blank	blank
01	01	01	0 0 0 0 1	A	1
02	02	02	0 0 0 1 0	E	2
03	03	03	0 0 0 1 1	/	1/
04	04	04	0 0 1 0 0	Y	3
05	05	05	0 0 1 0 1	U	4
06	06	06	0 0 1 1 0	I	3/
07	07	07	0 0 1 1 1	O	5
08	08	10	0 1 0 0 0	fig blank	fig blank
09	09	11	0 1 0 0 1	J	6
10	0A	12	0 1 0 1 0	G	7
11	0B	13	0 1 0 1 1	H	'
12	0C	14	0 1 1 0 0	B	8
13	0D	15	0 1 1 0 1	C	9
14	0E	16	0 1 1 1 0	F	5/
15	0F	17	0 1 1 1 1	D	Ø
16	10	20	1 0 0 0 0	letr blnk	letr blnk
17	11	21	1 0 0 0 1	–	.
18	12	22	1 0 0 1 0	X	9/
19	13	23	1 0 0 1 1	Z	:
20	14	24	1 0 1 0 0	S	7/2
21	15	25	1 0 1 0 1	T	
22	16	26	1 0 1 1 0	W	?
23	17	27	1 0 1 1 1	V	!
24	18	30	1 1 0 0 0	erasure	erasure
25	19	31	1 1 0 0 1	K	(
26	1A	32	1 1 0 1 0	M	)
27	1B	33	1 1 0 1 1	L	=
28	1C	34	1 1 1 0 0	R	–
29	1D	35	1 1 1 0 1	Q	/
30	1E	36	1 1 1 1 0	N	£
31	1F	37	1 1 1 1 1	P	+

which were used by the British Post Office on a telegraph system invented by Baudot in 1874.

In an ordinary coding scheme five bits can represent at most 32 different characters. This is hardly enough for 26 letters, 10 digits, and some punctuation; therefore, devices using five-bit codes must operate in modes. When in the letters mode, received codes will be interpreted as letters. One code is reserved for switching to figures mode, and one is reserved for switching to letters mode. When in figures mode, received codes will be interpreted as figures or punctuation.

ASCII

The most widely used data code in North America is the seven bit *American Standard Code for Information Interchange* (ASCII) shown in Table 2-9. Unlike five bit codes, ASCII has sufficient codes available to represent uppercase, lowercase, numbers, and a generous set of punctuation and control characters. The various control characters are explained in Tables 2-10 and 2-11. ASCII is an approved standard of the American National Standard Institution. A slightly different seven bit code shown in Table 2-12 is defined as the international standard CCITT Alphabet No. 5.

EBCDIC

Many large mainframe computers, especially those made by IBM, use the eight bit *extended binary-coded decimal interchanged code* (EBCDIC) shown in Table 2-13.

Table 2-9. Seven Bit ASCII Code.

B_6		0	0	0	0	1	1	1	1
B_5		0	0	1	1	0	0	1	1
B_4		0	1	0	1	0	1	0	1
$B_3 B_2 B_1 B_0$		0	1	2	3	4	5	6	7
0 0 0 0	0	NUL	DLE	SP	0	@	P	`	p
0 0 0 1	1	SOH	DC1	!	1	A	Q	a	q
0 0 1 0	2	STX	DC2	"	2	B	R	b	r
0 0 1 1	3	ETX	DC3	#	3	C	S	c	s
0 1 0 0	4	EOT	DC4	$	4	D	T	d	t
0 1 0 1	5	ENQ	NAK	%	5	E	U	e	u
0 1 1 0	6	ACK	SYN	&	6	F	V	f	v
0 1 1 1	7	BEL	ETB	'	7	G	W	g	w
1 0 0 0	8	BS	CAN	(	8	H	X	h	x
1 0 0 1	9	HT	EM	)	9	I	Y	i	y
1 0 1 0	10	LF	SUB	*	:	J	Z	j	z
1 0 1 1	11	VT	ESC	+	;	K	[	k	{
1 1 0 0	12	FF	FS	,	<	L	\	l		
1 1 0 1	13	CR	GS	-	=	M	]	m	}
1 1 1 0	14	SO	RS	.	>	N	^	n	~
1 1 1 1	15	SI	US	/	?	O	_	o	DEL

Table 2-10. ASCII Communications Control Characters.

SOH-Start of Heading-used to indicate the beginning of the header portion of a message. If header is divided into blocks, SOH is also used at the beginning of each block.

STX-Start of Text-used to separate the header and text portions of a message. If a header is not used, STX simply indicates the beginning of the message. If the text portion of the message is divided into blocks, STX is also used at the beginning of each block.

ETX-End of Text-used to indicate the end of the text portion of a message.

EOT-End of Transmission-used to indicate: 1. normal termination of a transmission; 2. aborted transmission; 3. request from a slave station for the master to abort transmission.

ETB-End of Transmission Block-used to indicate the end of a block of transmitted data. If a block check code is used, it immediately follows ETB.

ENQ-Enquiry-used to request a response from another station. The exact type of response requested will depend on the protocol and usage context.

ACK-Acknowledge-used as an affirmative reply. Usually used to acknowledge successful receipt of a block of data.

NAK-Negative Acknowledge-used as a negative reply. Usually used to indicate that an error was detected in a received block of data.

SYN-Synchronous Idle-used in synchronous systems to establish and maintain character syncronism.

DLE-Data Link Escape-used to indicate that a limited number (determined by protocol in use) of subsequent characters are to be interpretted as supplemental controls and not as data.

ERROR DETECTION

Character parity is a simple and widely used error detection scheme in which an extra bit is added to each character. For even parity, the value of the extra bit is set so that the total number of ONE bits in each character is always even. Likewise, for odd parity the extra bit is set to make the total number of ONE bits in each character odd. Thus, whenever a single bit error occurs anywhere in a character changing a ONE into a ZERO or changing a ZERO into a ONE, the parity sense of the character will be changed and the receiving device will be able to detect that an error has occurred. In fact, parity checking will detect any error condition which

17

corrupts an odd number of bits in any character. *Longitudinal parity* is similar to character parity except instead of adding extra bits to each character, an extra character called the *block check character* (BCC) is added to each block of data. The value of each bit in the BCC will be determined by the number of ONEs in the corresponding bit position of each character in the block. This may sound confusing, but as shown in Fig. 2-1, it's really very simple. Character parity is sometimes called *vertical redundancy check* (VRC), and longitudinal parity is sometimes called *longitudinal redundancy check* (LRC). Figure 2-2 shows how VRC and LRC can be used together as *block parity* which can detect exactly which bit has been corrupted. Despite its usefulness, parity does suffer from the limitation of being unable to detect an even number of bit errors. This problem can be virtually eliminated by using a different error detection scheme called *cyclic redundancy checking* (CRC).

CYCLIC REDUNDANCY CHECKING

Error detection with cyclic redundancy checking is based on the fact that an N-bit message can be treated as an N-bit binary number or as an N-th order polynomial which can be divided by a *generator polynomial* to produce a quotient and a remainder. This remainder is then appended to the message and transmitted. At the receiver, another remainder will be computed from the received data bits and compared to

Table 2-11. ASCII Special Characters.

NUL-Null	**DC1**-Device Control 1
BEL-Bell	**DC2**-Device Control 2
BS-Backspace	**DC3**-Device Control 3
HT-Horizontal Tab	**DC4**-Device Control 4
LF-Line Feed	**EM**-End of Medium
VT-Vertical Tab	**SUB**-Substitute
FF-Form Feed	**ESC**-Escape
CR-Carriage Return	**FS**-File Separator
SO-Shift Out	**GS**-Group Separator
SI-Shift In	**RS**-Record Separator
CAN-Cancel	**US**-Unit Separator

Table 2-12. CCITT Alphabet #5.

B3 B2 B1 B0		0	1	2	3	4	5	6	7
B6		0	0	0	0	1	1	1	1
B5		0	0	1	1	0	0	1	1
B4		0	1	0	1	0	1	0	1
0 0 0 0	0	NUL	TC7	SP	0	@	P	`	p
0 0 0 1	1	TC1	DC1	!	1	A	Q	a	q
0 0 1 0	2	TC2	DC2	"	2	B	R	b	r
0 0 1 1	3	TC3	DC3	#	3	C	S	c	s
0 1 0 0	4	TC4	DC4	¤	4	D	T	d	t
0 1 0 1	5	TC5	TC8	%	5	E	U	e	u
0 1 1 0	6	TC6	TC9	&	6	F	V	f	v
0 1 1 1	7	BEL	TC10	'	7	G	W	g	w
1 0 0 0	8	FE0	CAN	(	8	H	X	h	x
1 0 0 1	9	FE1	EM	)	9	I	Y	i	y
1 0 1 0	10	FE2	SUB	*	:	J	Z	j	z
1 0 1 1	11	FE3	ESC	+	;	K	[	k	{
1 1 0 0	12	FE4	IS4	,	<	L	\	l	|
1 1 0 1	13	FE5	IS3	-	=	M	]	m	}
1 1 1 0	14	SO	IS2	.	>	N	^	n	-
1 1 1 1	15	SI	IS1	/	?	O	_	o	DEL

Table 2-13. EBCDIC Eight Bit Code.

B3 B2 B1 B0																
B7	0	0	0	0	0	0	0	0	1	1	1	1	1	1	1	1
B6	0	0	0	0	1	1	1	1	0	0	0	0	1	1	1	1
B5	0	0	1	1	0	0	1	1	0	0	1	1	0	0	1	1
B4	0	1	0	1	0	1	0	1	0	1	0	1	0	1	0	1
0 0 0 0	NUL	DLE			SP	&	-						{	}	\	0
0 0 0 1	SOH	DC1					/		a	j	¬		A	J		1
0 0 1 0	STX	DC2	SYN						b	k	s		B	K	S	2
0 0 1 1	ETX	DC3							c	l	t		C	L	T	3
0 1 0 0									d	m	u		D	M	U	4
0 1 0 1	HT		LF						e	n	v		E	N	V	5
0 1 1 0		BS	ETB	EOT					f	o	w		F	O	W	6
0 1 1 1	DEL		ESC	EOT					g	p	x		G	P	X	7
1 0 0 0		CAN							h	q	y		H	Q	Y	8
1 0 0 1		EM						`	i	r	z		I	R	Z	9
1 0 1 0					[	]	|	:								
1 0 1 1	VT				.	$	,	#								
1 1 0 0	FF	FS		DC4	<	*	%	@								
1 1 0 1	CR	GS	ENQ	NAK	(	)	_	'								
1 1 1 0	SO	RS	ACK		+	;	>	=								
1 1 1 1	SI	US	BEL	SUB	!	^	?	■								

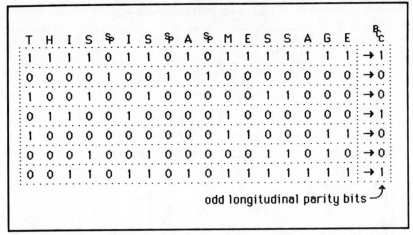

Fig. 2-1. Longitudinal parity.

the received remainder. If errors have occurred during transmission, the two remainder values will not agree. Careful selection of the generator polynomial will yield a very effective error detection scheme which outperforms parity in the detection of multibit or burst errors. There are three standard generator polynomials currently in use—*CRC-12, CRC-16,* and *CRC-CCITT.* The first generates a twelve-bit remainder and the other two generate sixteen-bit remainders. Some applications that require increased error protection use a 32-bit CRC. The actual implementation of the remainder generator is relatively simple—just a few shift registers and exclusive-

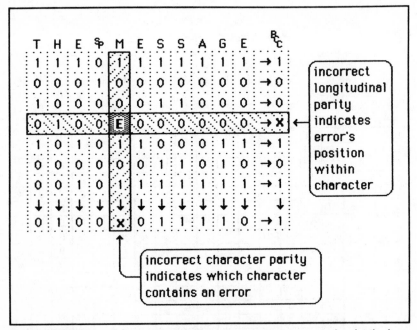

Fig. 2-2. Longitudinal parity and character parity used together can pinpoint the location of single bit errors.

OR gates. Implementations of the three common CRC schemes are shown in Fig. 2-3. Initially the register set is cleared and the message data is shifted in serially. After the last bit has been input the register set will contain the CRC remainder term.

DATA COMPRESSION

A data communications channel of any particular capacity can be used more efficiently if the data is first compressed so that fewer bits are required to transmit the same information. *Recurrence coding*, illustrated in Fig. 2-4, is one commonly used data compression technique in which the sending system replaces strings of three or more identical characters with special sequences. Each sequence consists of a special character, a character count, and one of the original characters. Upon detecting the special character, the receiving system will know to replace the sequence with the specified number of copies of the original character. Recurrence coding is particularly effective for compressing text such as source program files, which usually contain long strings of spaces and zeros.

Huffman coding is a technique suitable for compressing data, such as English

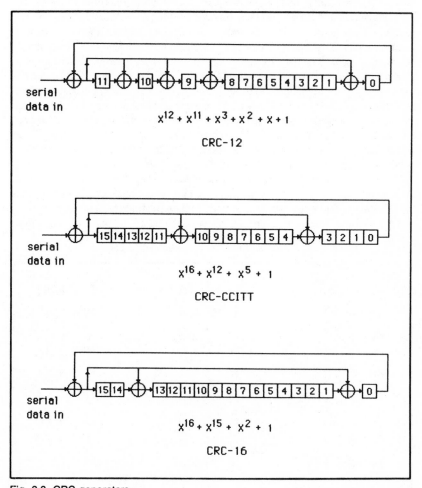

Fig. 2-3. CRC generators.

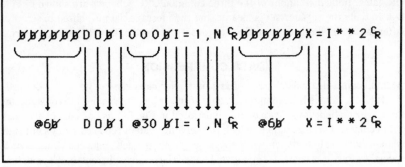

Fig. 2-4. Recurrence coding.

text, that contains a mix of different characters occurring in fairly predictable proportions. Codes with a fixed number of bits per character will require at least five bits to form sufficient code words to represent a complete single-case alphabet. However, economics can be realized by using short code words to represent frequently used characters and leaving the longer codes for the rarer ones. The frequent appearance of the shorter codes will tend to reduce the average character length well below five bits. The relative frequencies of characters in single case English text are listed in Table 2-14. One example of a Huffman code, listed in Table 2-15, will produce an average character length of 4.19 bits when used to encode typical English text. Careful examination of Table 2-15 will reveal an important characteristic of Huffman codes—the shorter codes never appear as the beginning bits of the longer codes. This is necessary, since the receiving device does not know the length of each incoming character. As soon as a bit pattern corresponding to a valid character is detected, the receiver will declare that this character has been received and will then begin collecting the bits to form the next character. The variable length of Huffman codes does unfortunately make them very sensitive to bit errors—rather than just garbling a single character a bit error can destroy an entire message. Therefore practical Huffman codes must usually incorporate reliable error detection and/or correction measures. Thus the code shown in Table 2-15 is only of theoretical

Table 2-14. Relative Character Frequencies in English Text.

E	2.85	D	3.94	B	1.41
T	9.40	L	3.64	W	1.40
A	7.74	C	3.22	V	1.00
0	7.73	U	2.80	K	0.40
N	7.23	F	2.75	X	0.38
R	7.23	M	2.69	Q	0.16
I	6.98	P	2.40	J	0.16
S	6.29	G	1.76	Z	0.10
H	4.61	Y	1.73		

Table 2-15. Example of a Huffman Code.

E	100	D	00100	B	101000
T	110	L	00101	W	101001
A	0000	C	01101	V	111111
O	0001	U	10101	K	11111000
N	0100	F	10110	X	11111001
R	0011	M	10111	Q	11111010
I	0101	P	11110	J	111110110
S	0111	G	011000	Z	111110111
H	1110	Y	011001		

interest—practical Huffman codes must incorporate some redundancy which will increase the average character length.

DATA ENCRYPTION

Codes or cyphers designed for privacy and security have been used in communications for centuries. It is perhaps fitting that data communications provides one of the largest uses of cryptographic techniques, since these techniques have been elevated to new heights by computers and digital technology. Data encryption techniques range from the simple to the sophisticated. In principle an effective cypher system can be implemented in a small computer system by simply adding a pseudorandom number to each byte of data before it is transmitted. The receiving system simply uses an identical random number generator using the same seed to generate the same pseudorandom number, which can then be subtracted from the received value to yield the original byte of data. Such a scheme would not withstand scrutiny by a professional cryptanalyst, but it would protect disk recordings of a private diary from curious amateurs. Cryptosystems designed to protect national defense information are both highly sophisticated and highly classified. Private and commercial users, however, can choose from either the National Bureau of Standards *Data Encryption Standard* (DES) or one of the several *public key* encryption schemes which have been proposed recently. The theory of these public key systems has been developed and published, but so far they have not been developed into commercial products. Therefore, anyone opting to use a public key system should be prepared to "go it alone" as far as construction of a working implementation is concerned. On the other hand, the DES was expressly developed as a common standard to be used throughout the commercial world and nondefense areas of the government. In the references are listed a number of sources that contain detailed information concerning the theory and implementation of DES and public key encryption schemes.

Chapter 3

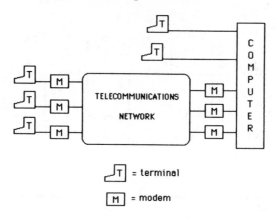

$\boxed{\small\square\!T}$ = terminal

$\boxed{\small M}$ = modem

Basics of Digital Signal Transmission

I N DISCUSSIONS OF DIGITAL LOGIC CIRCUITS, DIGITAL SIGNALS ARE OFTEN REPRE-
sented as idealized two-level waveforms with instantaneous transitions between
levels as shown in Fig. 3-1. In situations involving low speed, noise-free signals
transmitted over short distances, this approximate representation is more than adequate. Analysis involving high-speed logic, noisy signal conditions, or longer transmission distances, however, will require more accurate signal descriptions such as shown
in Fig. 3-2. In this picture several deviations from the ideal case can be seen. Instead of just two levels there is a range of possible levels due to added random noise.
The transitions are not instantaneous and the bits exhibit width variations or *jitter*.
Furthermore, there is a certain amount of *overshoot* and *ringing* at the end of each
transition. Analysis of such signals and the circuits that generate and propagate them
involves techniques of network and linear system analysis. These subjects alone could
fill volumes, but the basic idea is that electric circuits such as amplifiers and filters
can be characterized in three different but related ways—impulse response, step response, and frequency response. From these basic responses, a circuit's output or
response can be determined for virtually any input signal. In basic data communications analysis the impulse response is generally of less direct use than the step and
frequency responses. In this chapter we will look at step response and frequency
response analysis and then examine various types of digital signal waveforms along
with some of the practical difficulties encountered in trying to transmit them over
media such as telephone wiring, twisted pair wiring, coaxial cable, and fiberoptic
cable.

STEP RESPONSE

A *unit step*, shown in Fig. 3-3, has a value of zero for all time before turn-on and

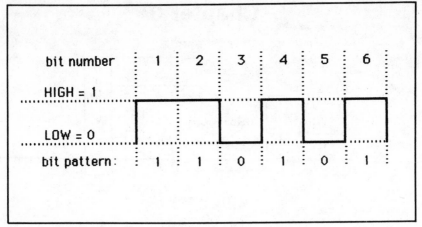

Fig. 3-1. Idealized digital signal waveform.

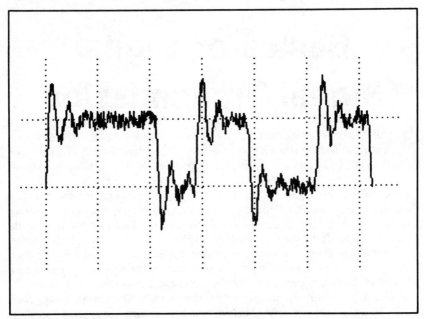

Fig. 3-2. Detailed view of a digital signal showing jitter, overshoot, ringing, and added noise.

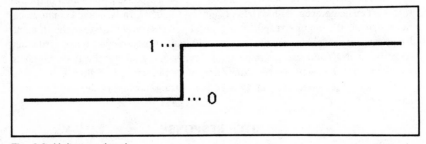

Fig. 3-3. Unit step signal.

a value of one for all time after turn-on. The outputs produced by some typical lowpass circuits in response to unit step inputs are shown in Fig. 3-4. A sequence of rectangular data pulses can be formed by summing a number of weighted and shifted unit steps as shown in Fig. 3-5. A linear system's output response to such an input can be found by forming a sum of similarly weighted and shifted step responses as shown in Fig. 3-6. Direct analysis using of the step response is generally limited to situations involving rectangular or nearly rectangular data pulses. *Frequency response* is a more general technique that can be used to analyze situations involving rectangular or nonrectangular pulses.

FREQUENCY RESPONSE

A periodic signal such as an alternating one-zero serial data stream can be mathematically broken down into a sum of *sine* and *cosine* waves. Such a summation is called a *Fourier series*. The sinusoids will have frequencies that correspond to the original signal's fundamental frequency and its harmonics. Sine cosine waves are simply sine waves phase shifted by one quarter of a cycle (i.e., 90° or $\pi/2$ radians), the sine and cosine components at each frequency can be combined into a single sinusoid which has a relative phase that depends on the ratio between the strengths of the sine and cosine components. Skipping the mathematical complexities, the bottom line is that a periodic rectangular pulse train will have a magnitude spectrum as shown in Fig. 3-7.

At the expense of even more complicated math, the Fourier series can be ex-

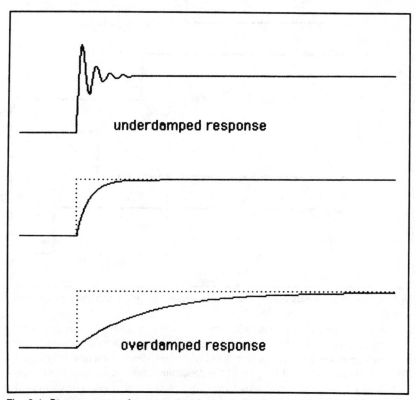

Fig. 3-4. Step response of some typical lowpass circuits.

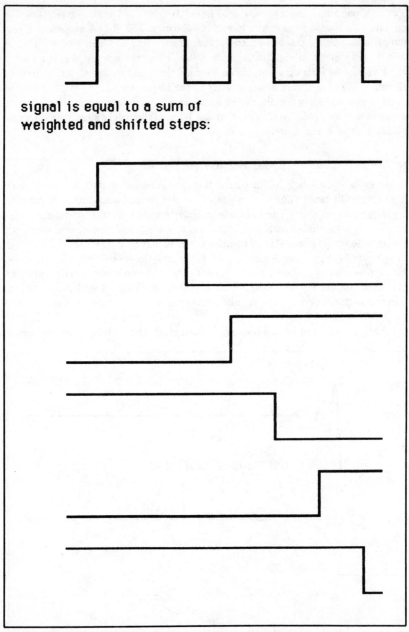

signal is equal to a sum of
weighted and shifted steps:

Fig. 3-5. Rectangular data pulses formed by summing weighted and shifted unit steps.

tended to the *Fourier transform*, which can be used to resolve virtually any signal of practical interest into sinusoidal components. There are a few differences. While the series produces a spectrum composed of discrete lines occurring only at harmonics of the fundamental frequency, the spectrum produced by transform analysis will, in general, exist over a continuous range of frequencies. The continuous spectrum of a single rectangular pulse appears in Fig. 3-8. As shown in Fig. 3-9,

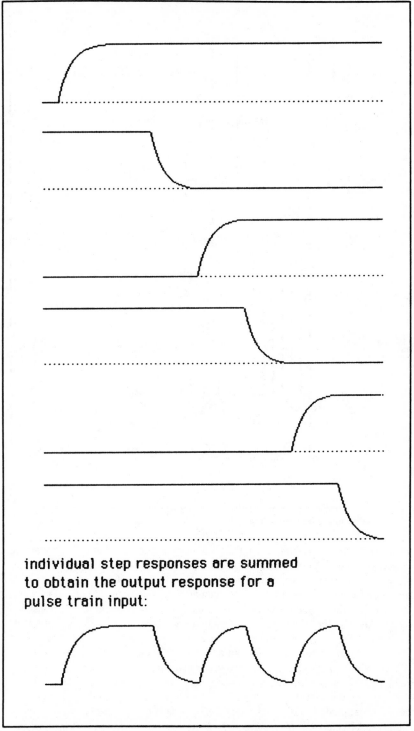

individual step responses are summed
to obtain the output response for a
pulse train input:

Fig. 3-6. Output response formed by summing weighted and shifted step responses.

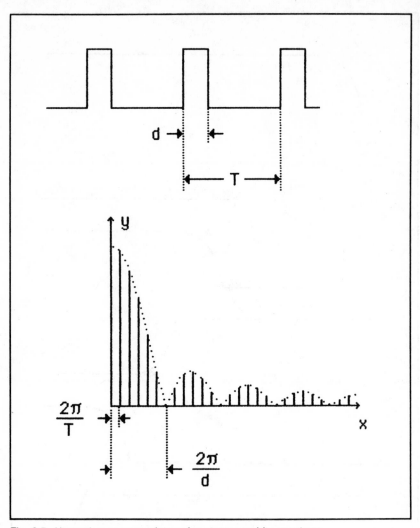

Fig. 3-7. Alternating one-zero data pulse stream and its spectrum.

an arbitrary train of rectangular pulses will have a spectrum that falls somewhere in between the discrete line spectrum of a periodic pulse train and the continous spectrum of a single pulse. Notice however that the shape of the envelope remains the same for all of these ospectra. Mathematically, this shape is defined as a *sinc function*, and the location of the *zeros* or *nulls* depends only on the width of a single pulse. (Actually the lobes of a since function are alternately positive and negative as shown in Fig. 3-10, but it is conventional in frequency spectra to show the negative lobes as positive magnitudes with an additional 180 degrees of phase shift.)

The ability to resolve signals into sinusoidal components is particularly useful since for a sinusoidal input, a linear system such as an amplifier or a filter will produce an output sinusoid of the same frequency as the input. The only changes will be in the amplitude and/or the phasing. Therefore a circuit's response to an arbitrary input can be computed by resolving the input into sinusoids via Fourier analysis, computing the corresponding output component for each sinusoidal component of

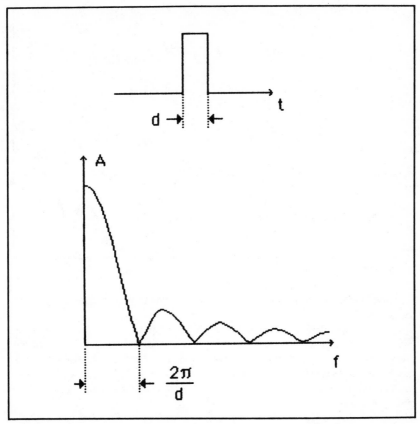

Fig. 3-8. Single frequency rectangular pulse and its continuous frequency spectrum.

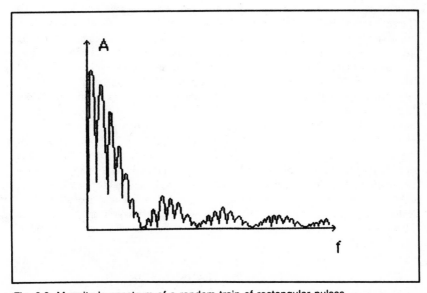

Fig. 3-9. Magnitude spectrum of a random train of rectangular pulses.

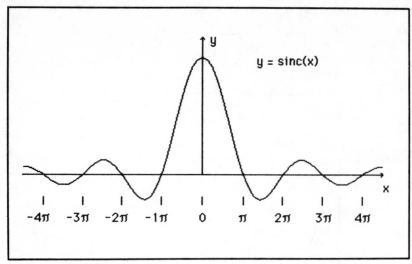

Fig. 3-10. Sinc function.

the input, and finally recombining the output sinusoids by means of inverse Fourier techniques.

Just as a signal's sinusoidal content at various frequencies is expressed as a frequency spectrum, a circuit's response to sinusoids of various frequencies can be expressed as a *frequency response*, which not surprisingly has two parts—a *magnitude response* and a *phase response*. For a linear system, the spectrum of the output can be obtained by simply multiplying the spectrum of the input by the system's frequency response at each frequency.

TRANSISTOR-TRANSISTOR LOGIC

Transistor-transistor logic or TTL is probably the most popular and widely used form of logic circuitry in the world today. Most computers and peripherals contain TTL circuits and often very short-range data communications can be accomplished using only this without having to resort to special purpose driver and receiver devices.

The internal circuitry of a typical TTL NAND gate is shown in Fig. 3-11. To produce a LOW output, Q3 is driven into cutoff and Q4 into saturation. This will cause the output pin to be pulled low with current from any external connections flowing to ground through Q4. Conversely, to produce a HIGH output, Q3 is driven into saturation and Q4 into cutoff. This will cause the output pin to be pulled high with current supplied to external loads through Q3 and D1. The output structure composed of Q3, Q4, and D1 is often referred to as a *totem pole output*. The voltage for a HIGH output is typically around +2.4 volts and for a LOW around +0.4 volts. Since outputs from TTL devices are usually used as inputs to other TTL devices, and since some deviation or noise corruption of the output voltages may occur, TTL devices are designed to interpret as a LOW any input voltage from ground up to +0.8 volts. Likewise any input voltage from +2.0 volts to +5.0 volts will be interpreted as a HIGH input.

UNBALANCED TRANSMISSION

Figure 3-12 shows an *unbalanced* data transmission scheme that can use TTL devices as drivers and receivers. When equipped with other types of drivers and receivers, unbalanced transmission is used in popular interfacing standards such as RS-232C and RS-423. In such a scheme, each signal circuit consists of one signal conductor and a ground return. Sometimes each circuit has its own ground return, and sometimes a single-ground conductor is shared by all circuits in the interface. The voltages on the signal lines are referenced to ground. Although this approach can reduce cabling requirements, the signal conductors can act like an antenna both radiating signal energy and receiving ambient rf energy from the surround area. For short cable runs in relatively benign environments this is frequently not a serious problem, but for longer cables or more severe rf environments the antenna-like behavior of the signal conductors can make unbalanced transmission schemes unusable.

When energy is radiated from the cable, several basic problems can arise. First, the radiated energy is lost and is not available to drive the receiver inputs at the far end of the cable. This limits the maximum allowable distance between the driver and receiver. Since the radiated signals can be quite strong in the immediate vicinity of the offending conductor, other nearby conductors are likely to act as receiving antennas and pick up these signals. This condition is referred to as *crosstalk*. In some cases the unintentional radiation can be strong enough to interfere with the operation of nearby radio and television receivers. The Federal Communications Commission (FCC) takes a dim view of such things and requires that all new models of digital equipment be tested in an attempt to prevent such situations. However, even if all the equipment in a system complies with FCC requirements, an interference problem can still be created by the cabling.

If the signal conductor acts as a receiving antenna, a wide variety of undesired

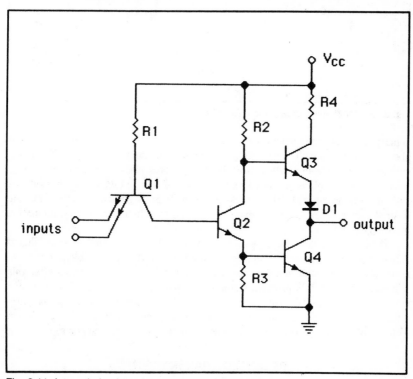

Fig. 3-11. Internal circuitry of a typical TTL NAND gate.

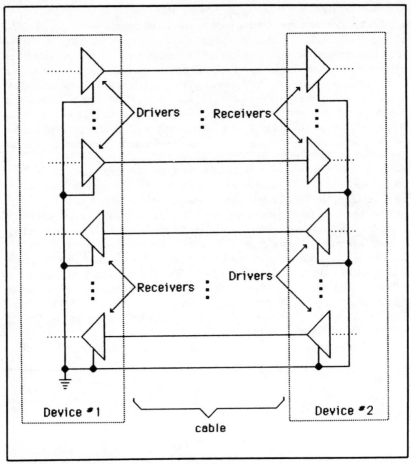

Fig. 3-12. Unbalanced data transmission scheme.

signals and noise can appear at the far end receiver inputs. This can include just about any rf signals in the conductor's surrounding environment—radio and TV broadcasts; brush noise from nearby motors; lightning strikes; and as mentioned previously, crosstalk from neighboring signal conductors. As shown in Fig. 3-13, if the voltages and currents produced by these undesired signals are significant compared to the desired signal, the receiver will make errors as it tries to interpret the combination of voltages and currents present at its input.

The use of shielded cable is one approach for combatting antenna effects of digital signal conductors. If one overall shield is used around the entire cable, the rf problems between the cable and the outside environment can be reduced; but often this will make the crosstalk problem worse. If a separate shield is placed around each conductor, the crosstalk problem can also be minimized, but such an approach requires cabling which can become prohibitively expensive. An alternative solution to the problem lies in the use of a balanced data transmission scheme.

BALANCED TRANSMISSION

Figure 3-14 shows a balanced transmission scheme which is used in the RS-422 in-

34

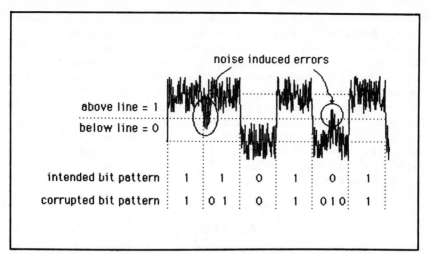

Fig. 3-13. Digital waveform showing bit errors induced by noise.

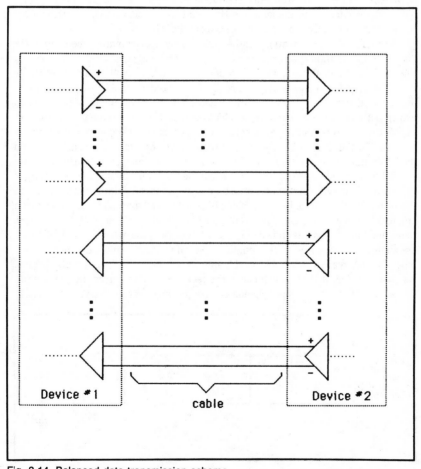

Fig. 3-14. Balanced data transmission scheme.

terfacing scheme. As shown, each signal circuit consists of a pair of conductors and the signal consists of a differential voltage between the two conductors. The voltage (with respect to ground) on one conductor of the pair will be mirrored or balanced by a voltage of equal magnitude but opposite polarity on the other conductor. Usually (but not always) the two conductors in a particular signal circuit will be twisted together to form a *twisted pair*. If a twisted pair is used for each circuit, the antenna effects so common in unbalanced transmission can be greatly reduced in the balanced approach. Any radiation from one conductor will tend to be cancelled by equal but opposite radiation from the other one in the pair. Any external rf which may be received by the conductors will be received in an almost identical form by both conductors in the pair. Because the receiver at the far end is looking for a voltage difference between the two conductors, it will ignore these *common mode* noise and interference signals.

LINE CAPACITANCE

The electrical conductors used for data transmission will always exhibit some resistance from one end to the other, and there will be a certain amount of capacitance between conductors and from each conductor to ground. This capacitance is completely distributed along the length of the conductors, and a precise mathematical representation requires the calculus of partial derivatives.

A simplified representation can be obtained by approximating the completely distributed capacitance as a number of discrete lumped capacitances as shown in Fig. 3-15. In an ideal communications line, the resistance and capacitance values would be zero and a square data pulse input to one end would result in a square pulse output from the other end. Unfortunately, practical communications lines do exhibit both resistance and capacitance. The combined effect of these two parameters causes the line to perform like a low-pass filter, producing nonsquare output pulses as shown in Fig. 3-16. The rise and fall times of the output pulses will depend on the line's time constant, which is equal to resistance times capacitance. The rise and fall times will be short for small values of the time constant and longer for larger values. Many practical communications lines will produce output pulses similar to those shown in Fig. 3-16. However some lines may also have significant inductance and leakage that will cause the output pulses to exhibit further distortion of their rising and falling edges as shown in Fig. 3-17. If the lengths of the rise and fall times are significant compared to the length of the pulses, the output response for one pulse may not reach a receivable level before the response for the next pulse begins. As shown in Fig. 3-18, this will cause the receiver to make errors in interpreting the output of the line. A similar phenomenon or just an incorrect setting of the thresh-

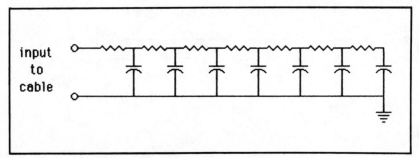

Fig. 3-15. Line capacitance approximated as discrete capacitors.

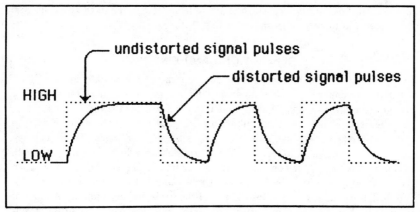

Fig. 3-16. Digital waveform showing long risetimes and falltimes caused by line capacitance.

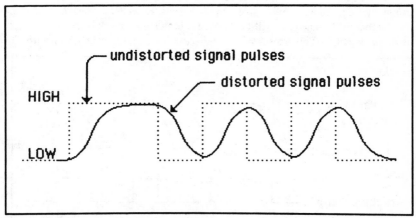

Fig. 3-17. Digital waveform showing pulse-edge distortion due to combined effects of line capacitance, inductance, and leakage.

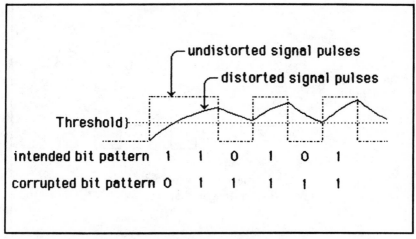

Fig. 3-18. Bit errors caused by severe pulse distortion.

old can cause *bias distortion,* which is a significant imbalance in the baud lengths for spaces and for marks as shown in Fig. 3-19.

REFLECTIONS AND RINGING

Referring to Fig. 3-20, assume that the output of driver A is initially in a low state. When the computer begins to send data to the printer, the output of the driver will change from low to high. Typically this transition will take several nanoseconds. However it may take from three to four nanoseconds per foot for such a change to travel down a length of wire. Thus, for a long cable there will a significant propagation delay from driver A to receiver B. The transient traveling down the cable will, of course, have a voltage component and a current component. The ratio between these two components will be determined by the *characteristic impedance* of the cable ($V/I = Z_o$). As the signal reaches the end of the cable and encounters the input of receiver B, there may be some difficulties. In the input stage of receiver B the voltage/current ratio is determined by the input impedance ($V/I = Z_{in}$). If the impedances of the cable and the receiver input are equal, then the signal will pass painlessly from the end of the cable into receiver B. However if these impedances are not matched then there will be an excess of current or voltage which cannot be accommodated. This excess will be reflected back up the cable toward driver

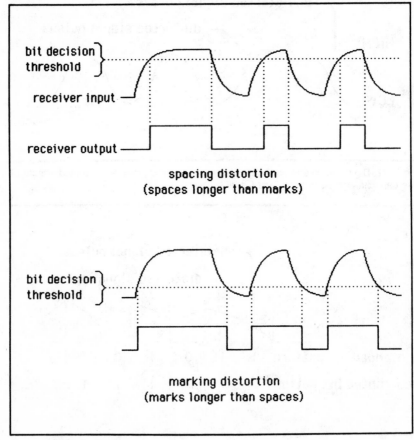

Fig. 3-19. Bias distortion.

38

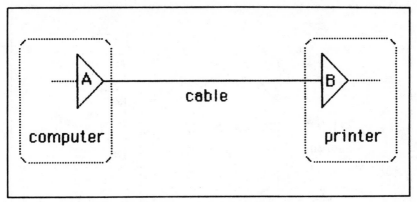

Fig. 3-20. Transmitting data from a computer to a printer.

A. Again, if the output stage impedance Z_{out} of driver A is not equal to Z_o, some of this reflection will be rereflected back towards B. Repeated reflections will continue until all of the energy originally output from driver A is dissipated. These reflections can add or subtract from the original signal depending on the relationship between the various impedances. For efficient transfer of energy into the cable, Z_{out} of driver A will usually be smaller than Z_o of the cable. If this is the case and if Z_{in} of receiver B is large compared to Z_o, overshoot and ringing as shown in Fig. 3-21 will result. If Z_{in} is small compared to Z_o, the receiver will load down the cable and require that it be driven at high levels in order to maintain an acceptable signal level at the receiver input. This will waste power and can require the use of cable having heavier conductors and insulation. Either of these conditions can lead to errors in the received data. A careful matching of Z_o and Z_{in} is needed to avoid ringing or excessive cable loading.

UNBALANCED TRANSMISSION USING TTL

Figure 3-22 shows a relatively simple unbalanced data transmission scheme which can be implemented using 7407 open collector drivers, twisted pair cabling, and a

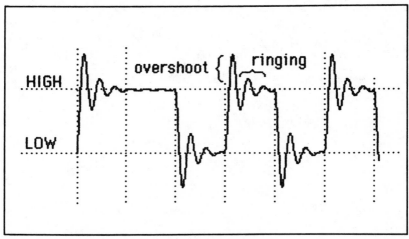

Fig. 3-21. Digital waveform showing overshoot and ringing.

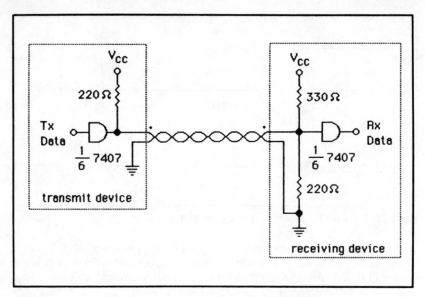

Fig. 3-22. A simple unbalanced transmission scheme using TTL.

few pullup and terminating resistors. This scheme can be used quite effectively to interface a variety of devices when you have control over both the driver and receiver design. In most cases, however, one end will already be defined and the other end must be designed to be compatible with it. Typically, in the small computer arena this will involve designing to one of the established standards such as RS-232C, RS-422, or RS-423, which will be discussed in Chapters 7 and 8.

Chapter 4

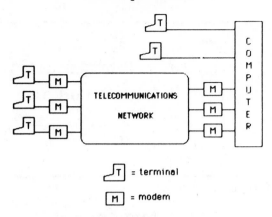

$\boxed{\mathrm{T}}$ = terminal

$\boxed{M}$ = modem

Timing and Synchronization of Digital Signals

I N MOST DATA COMMUNICATIONS SCHEMES THE DATA IS TRANSMITTED SERIAL-ly over a single link as shown in Fig. 4-1. This is in contrast to bussing schemes as in Fig. 4-2 in which all the bits in each character, byte, or word are transmitted in parallel. Serial communications can be either *asynchronous* or *synchronous*. In asynchronous communications the machine that transmits the data and the machine which receives it as the other end use independent clock signals that are not synchronized with each other. In synchronous communications the transmitting and receiving machines use a common clock signal which is either imbedded in the data or sent along with the data via a separate circuit.

ASYCHRONOUS DATA COMMUNICATIONS

Consider a 150 baud datalink in which the transmitter clock is running one percent fast and the receiver clock is running one percent slow. In two seconds the transmitter will send out 303 bits, but the receiver will only interpret them as 297 bits—clearly intolerable error rates will result. Asynchronous communication uses start and stop bits on each character as shown in Fig. 4-3 to combat this problem. An idle transmitter will send a continuous HIGH or mark. When it is ready to start sending a character, it will begin by sending a start bit that consists of one space. Then comes five to eight data bits (depending on the particular data code being used—see Chapter 2) followed by a parity bit. (For a discussion of parity see Chapter 2.) The transmitter will then end the character with a stop that consists of a HIGH or mark, which is either 1, 1.5, or 2 bits long. The transmitter can then either send the start for the next character or extend the stop mark indefinitely to idle.

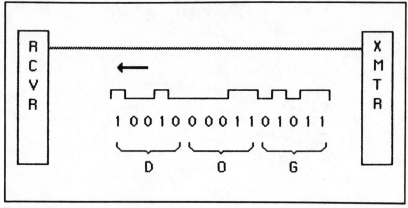

Fig. 4-1. Serial data communications.

UARTs

Asynchronous communications protocols were originally developed to support communication via teletype machines, but modern terminal equipment that communicates asynchronously usually employs a *universal asynchronous receiver/transmitter* or *UART*.

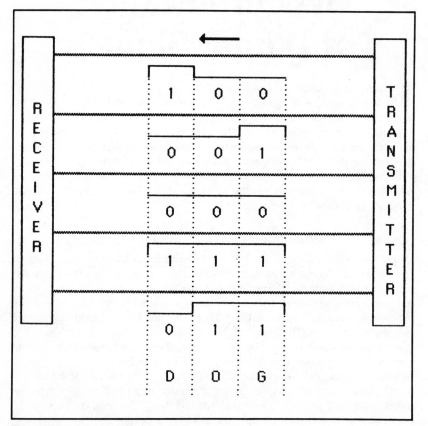

Fig. 4-2. Parallel data communications.

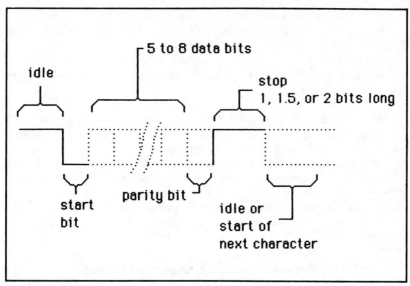

Fig. 4-3. Character format for asynchronous communications.

A very simplified block diagram of typical UART transmitter operation is shown in Fig. 4-4. The transmitter section of the UART accepts parallel data (5 to 8 bits) from the computer or terminal and loads it into a shift register in response to the LOAD DATA input. The data is then shifted by one bit for each cycle of the XMIT CLK input. The line driver for the serial output line is connected to bit zero of the shift register and a new bit value is output each time a shift occurs. An actual UART transmitter is somewhat more complex, having additional features such as:

- A double or sometimes triple parallel input buffer to make CPU servicing of the UART less time-critical;
- A XMIT BUFFER EMPTY flag output to indicate when all of the input buffers are empty;
- A XMIT END-OF-CHAR flag to indicate that a character has been transmit-

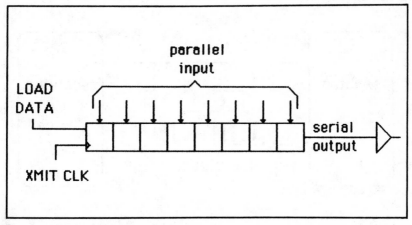

Fig. 4-4. UART transmitter operation.

43

ted and that space is now available in the input buffer for another character;

 ● A set of input lines that allow programming the number of bits (i.e., 5, 6, 7, or 8) to be transmitted for each character;

 ● Parity generation logic with an input line to select even or odd parity; and

 ● An input to allow programming the length of the stop bit appended to each transmitted character.

When waiting for the start of a new character, the receiver section of the UART searches data coming in on the serial input line for a high-to-low transition indicating the beginning of a start bit. When this transition is found, the UART then counts off one half of a bit time and samples the serial input line. If the sampled signal is low, the UART assumes reception of a valid start bit and begins counting off bit times and sampling the serial input line at approximately the center of each bit cell. When a complete character has been correctly received the UART will transfer the assembled character into a received data register and assert a "received-data available" flag.

SYNCHRONOUS DATA COMMUNICATIONS

In the most basic synchronous communications scheme, a clock signal is transmitted along with the data via a separate circuit as shown in Fig. 4-5. Since both the transmitter and receiver use the same clock the problem of accumulated differences between clocks does not occur and data can be sent continuously without any need for inserting start and stop bits. Although the common clock solves the problem of bit alignment, we must still face the problem of character alignment or *framing*. Consider the data signal shown in Fig. 4-6. Depending on where the character boundaries are assumed to be, this data can be interpreted in a number of different ways. Traditionally this problem has been solved by using data codes that define synch characters that will not appear in normal data and whose bit pattern is unlikely to be duplicated by adjacent portions of any two other character codes appearing consecutively in normal data. Thus, when the receiver recognizes the synch pattern it can establish character boundaries with a high probability of being correct. For synchronous communications, a *universal synchronous receiver/transmitter* or *USRT* capable of recognizing synch characters is used in lieu of the asynchronous UART.

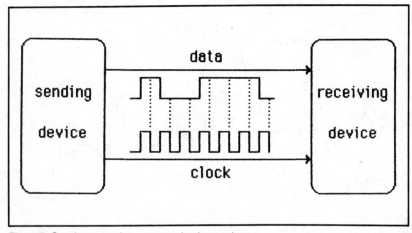

Fig. 4-5. Synchronous data communications scheme.

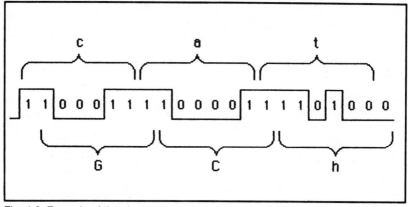

Fig. 4-6. Example of the character framing problem in synchronous serial data transmission.

CLOCK RECOVERY

Synchronous communication makes more efficient use of a data channel than does asynchronous, but this advantage is lost if a separate clock channel must be provided and maintained. Fortunately, a reasonably precise baud rate clock can be recovered directly from a synchronous data stream by means of a *phase-locked loop* (PLL) employed as a clock recovery circuit as shown in Fig. 4-7. Details of PLL design and operation are beyond the scope of this book, but design of workable loops does not require a complete knowledge of the subject. Some of the popular introductory PLL books are very superficial and concentrate primarily on experiments and demonstrations of the easiest concepts while neglecting some of the real world problems associated with the practical use of PLLs for recovery of data clocks. However there are several excellent references that are listed in the back of this book. Neglecting the gory details, the important thing to remember about PLL recovery is that it will not work if the level transitions in the data signal are too sparse. A typical baseband data signal is likely to contain long transition-free passages that could cause a clock recovery PLL to lose synchronization. Therefore, a number of *line codes* have

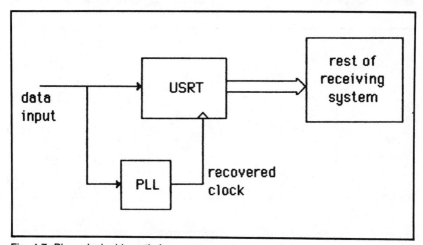

Fig. 4-7. Phase locked loop timing recovery.

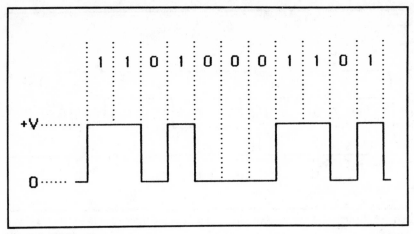

Fig. 4-8. NRZ coding.

been developed to ensure that the transmitted signal will contain sufficient transitions, regardless of the bit pattern being sent.

BASIC LINE CODES

Digital signals are typically translated or converted into particular formats for long-distance transmission. These formats are called *line codes* and are independent of the particular data code (e.g., ASCII, BCD, EBCDIC, etc.) being used. A number of line codes have been developed, each exhibiting particular advantages and disadvantages.

Nonreturn to zero or *NRZ* is the common digital data signal format in which logical zeros are represented by nominally zero signal levels and logical ones are represented by some nonzero signal level such as in TTL. As shown in Fig. 4-8, the signal level remains constant throughout the duration of each bit time, switching to a new level only at the beginning of a new bit of data. In the context of line coding, NRZ is sometimes also referred to as *unipolar* coding. While very simple and widely used within digital devices, NRZ has some serious drawbacks as a format for transmis-

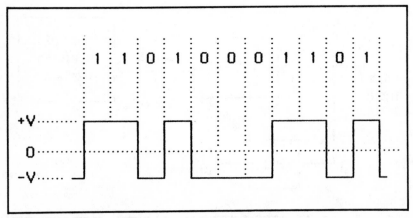

Fig. 4-9. Bipolar NRZ coding.

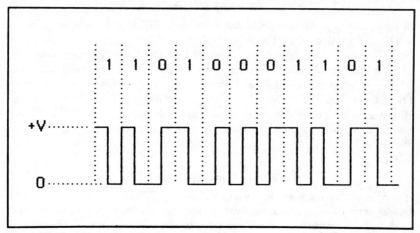

Fig. 4-10. Manchester II coding.

sion of data. If a long sequence of all zeros or all ones is transmitted in NRZ format, the signal will appear as a constant level. If the distant receiver is using a PLL to recover timing from the signal, such a constant level is likely to cause the PLL to lose lock with consequent errors in data extraction. Furthermore, most practical baseband data transmission networks are ac coupled using transformers or blocking capacitors to stop dc signal components. The dc signal level resulting from a long string of identical bits will not pass through such systems. Finally, unipolar line codes are wasteful of power, requiring twice the power of some other types of codes.

BIPOLAR CODING

Bipolar NRZ is a simple enhancement of NRZ coding that reduces the average power consumption by a factor of two. As shown in Fig. 4-9, a signal level equal in magnitude to the mark level but of opposite polarity is used instead of a zero signal level to represent spaces. While bipolar NRZ requires less power than unipolar NRZ, it still exhibits the problems of blocked dc components and timing loss due to long runs of all ones or all zeros.

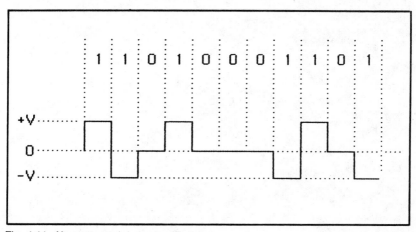

Fig. 4-11. Alternate mark inversion coding.

BIPHASE CODING

In *digital biphase* or *Manchester II* coding, shown in Fig. 4-10, a one is represented as a high-to-low signal transition occurring in the middle of the bit cell, while a zero is represented as a low-to-high transition. (Manchester II is sometimes loosely referred to simply as Manchester but strictly speaking this is incorrect as digital biphase is different from the long unused and forgotten original Manchester code.) Because a transition occurs in every bit cell, the problems of dc blocking and timing loss are eliminated. Manchester II is a very popular line code finding use in HDLC, SDLC, and Ethernet implementations as well as in many magnetic data recording applications.

ALTERNATE MARK INVERSION

A sample of *alternate mark inversion* (AMI) coding is shown in Fig. 4-11. Zero bits (spaces) are encoded as zero signal levels, and one bits (marks) are encoded as nonzero levels that alternate between positive and negative for successive marks. The reduced dc and low frequency content of AMI signals makes them well suited for ac coupled systems. AMI coding is used in T1 and T1C telephone carrier systems.

Chapter 5

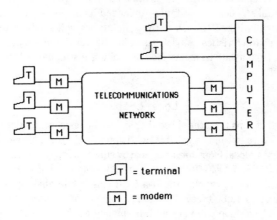

$$\boxed{\text{T}}$$ = terminal

$$\boxed{\text{M}}$$ = modem

Public
Telephone Networks

A SYSTEM DESIGNER CONCERNED WITH COMMUNICATION OF DIGITAL DATA IS generally limited to three major categories of transmission facility—private cabling, radio, and the public telephone network (PTN). PTN facilities can be further categorized into the switched voice network and leased line service. The switched voice network is the common everyday "dial up and talk" portion of the PTN. Although a huge amount of data is transmitted via the globe-spanning switched voice network; data rates, error performance, and terminal equipment complexity are often adversely affected by limitations and peculiarities of the network.

Leased line service is currently the major way of circumventing limitations in the switched voice network. Specific physical facilities of the network are selected, conditioned, augmented, and dedicated to support particular customers who are prepared to pay significantly higher rates for improved data transmission capabilities. In this chapter, we will be primarily concerned with the characteristics of the switched network since this represents a worst case and it is still the most used of all data transmission facilities. Data communication techniques developed to work on the switched network facilities are virtually guaranteed to work in private and leased line services which usually provide significant improvement over the switched network performance characteristics. Present technology is sufficiently advanced that the possible configurations and capabilities of totally private cabling systems are limited primarily by economic rather than technological constraints. At the end of this chapter, we will survey the various types of leased line service which are available from AT&T and the various local telco's that formerly were the Bell System. Specialized non-telco common-carrier data transmission services are also available, but since the market is so fluid any coverage of them in a book such as this one would quickly become obsolete.

LOOPS AND TRUNKS

In general, the telephone network connection between two users will involve three basic types of links. These three types—unloaded loops, loaded loops, and carrier trunks are shown in Fig. 5-1. Each of these link types will exhibit different distortion and noise characteristics. As discussed in Chapter 3, the important distortion characteristics from a data transmission viewpoint are attenuation, envelope delay, and phase shift.

Local Loops

The local loop that runs from the subscriber site to the telco local office will typically consist of a two-wire twisted pair that is tightly bundled into a cable along with many more pairs carrying local loops for other nearby subscribers. The conductor size will range from AWG 28 to AWG 16 or even larger, depending on the length of the loop and on the maximum allowable loss. If a 6 dB loss is tolerable, up to 11,700 feet of 26 gauge or up to 42,800 feet of 16 gauge copper can be used. The attenuation of a signal on a local loop will vary with frequency as shown in Fig. 5-2. A signal that contains many different frequency components, each attenuated by different amounts will exhibit attenuation distortion. The local loop is essentially a low-pass filter, attenuating high frequencies much more than lower frequencies. Low-pass filtering inherent in the telephone networks is what imparts that distinctive "telephone quality" to voice traffic. While not a serious impairment to conversation, attenuation distortion can cause problems for data transmission.

The envelope delay characteristic of typical loop is shown in Fig. 5-3. Ideally this should be flat over the range of frequencies contained in the signal to be transmitted. The effect of delay distortion on a baseband data signal is shown in Fig. 5-4. The most important impact of delay distortion, however, occurs in modulated signals as we will discover in Chapter 6.

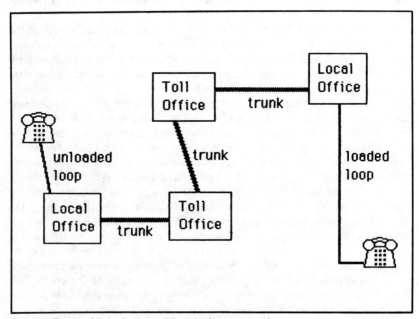

Fig. 5-1. Types of links in the public telephone network.

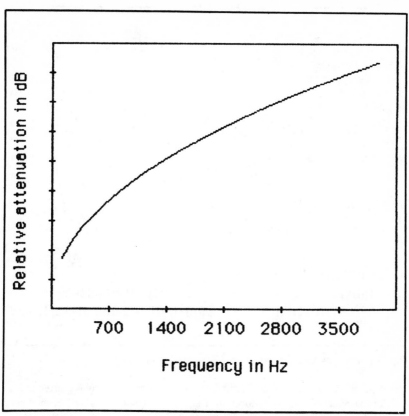

Fig. 5-2. Attenuation characteristic of a typical nonloaded local loop.

Loaded Loops

In order to minimize the distortion effects of line capacitance, telephone companies have frequently added inductance to the longer local loops and noncarrier trunks by inserting loading coils at intervals along the line. Attenuation characteristics for

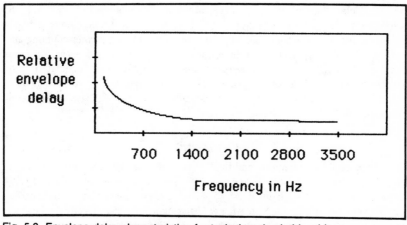

Fig. 5-3. Envelope delay characteristic of a typical nonloaded local loop.

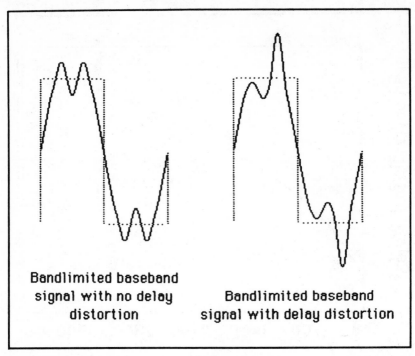

Bandlimited baseband
signal with no delay
distortion

Bandlimited baseband
signal with delay distortion

Fig. 5-4. Effect of delay distortion on a baseband data signal.

a typical loaded loop are shown in Fig. 5-5, and the envelope delay is plotted in Fig. 5-6. The attenuation is quite reduced for frequencies below about 2800 Hz and very greatly increased for frequencies above 3400 Hz. However, the envelope delay characteristic is greatly degraded.

Trunks

There are more than a dozen different carrier schemes used on trunks throughout the nationwide network, but they are all carefully engineered to provide similar characteristics for each and every voicegrade channel carried. The attenuation and envelope delay characteristics for a typical trunk are shown in Figs. 5-7 and 5-8, respectively. The important thing to notice here is that the attenuation is virtually infinite at very low frequencies. This is due primarily to transformer coupling and historical amplifier performance limitations. Because baseband signals contain relatively large amounts of low frequency energy, they must be modulated up to a higher frequency before being transmitted over carrier systems. The various modulation processes and specific modulator-demodulator (modem) designs will be discussed in Chapter 6.

SIGNALING

In order to establish, maintain, and finally take down connections between distant subscribers, the various participating telco offices must transmit status and call progress information among themselves. This can be accomplished by using separate signaling circuits or by using *in-band* or *out-band* signaling tones directly on the voice circuits. From a data transmission viewpoint the major concern is with in-band signal-

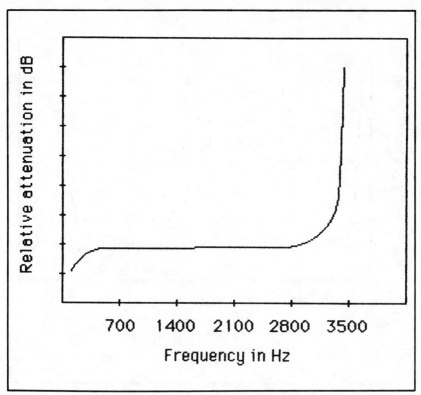

Fig. 5-5. Attenuation characteristic of a typical loaded loop.

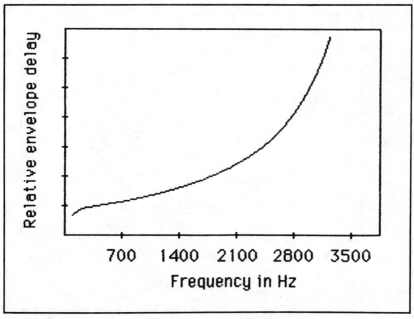

Fig. 5-6. Envelope delay characteristic of a typical loaded local loop.

53

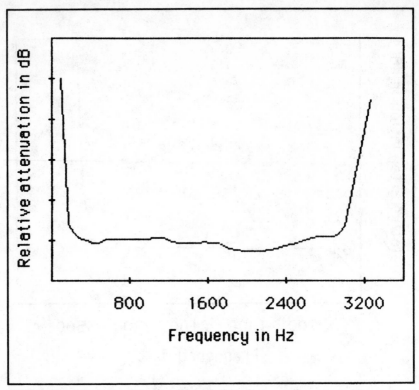

Fig. 5-7. Attenuation characteristic of a typical trunk.

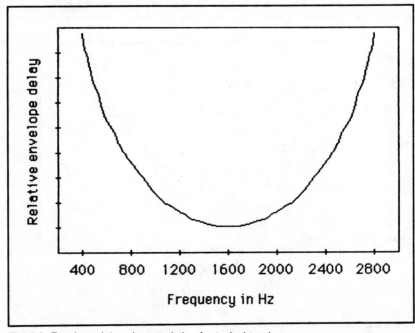

Fig. 5-8. Envelope delay characteristic of a typical trunk.

54

ing, since improperly designed data signals can appear to telco equipment as in-band signaling, thus causing improper operation of the telco equipment. To prevent this, modem designs must avoid the use of frequencies corresponding to the signaling tones used by telco equipment. Most North American interoffice signaling schemes use the tone assignments shown in Table 5-1. Furthermore, a very widespread single frequency signaling scheme employs 2600 Hz tones.

TOUCHTONE®

"Touchtone" is a registered trademark belonging to Ma Bell—the generic term used to refer to Touchtone type systems is "dual tone multifrequency" or DTMF. Unlike interoffice signaling, the frequencies used by DTMF pushbutton dialing systems do not necessarily have to be avoided. In fact, DTMF frequencies are used in some computer banking systems to allow transactions and balance inquiries to be made by simply keying in the appropriate information on the Touchtone pad of an ordinary telephone. The frequencies in the Touchtone DTMF scheme are listed in Table 5-2.

Table 5-1. Tone Assignments Used for Interoffice Signaling in North America.

Signal Meaning	Frequencies of Tone Pair	
KP1 (start of signaling for national call)	1100	1700
KP2 (start of signaling for international call)	1300	1700
Digits: 1	700	900
2	700	1100
3	900	1100
4	700	1300
5	900	1300
6	1100	1300
7	700	1500
8	900	1500
9	1100	1500
0	1300	1500
ST (end of signaling)	1500	1700

Table 5-2. Tone Assignments Used in Touchtone® DTMF System.

	"B" Frequency (Hz)		
	1209	1336	1477
"A" Frequency (Hz) 697	1	2	3
770	4	5	6
852	7	8	9
941	*	0	#

DIRECT CONNECTION REQUIREMENTS

Before 1968 it was illegal to connect anything other than AT&T equipment to Bell System telephone lines. Modems (Bell calls them datasets) and autodialing equipment had to be purchased, or more often, leased from Bell. In 1968 after the "Carter phone ruling" it became legal to connect non-telco equipment to the telephone lines as long as the actual connection was made through a telco supplied isolator called a *direct access adapter* (DAA). In 1976 the requirement to use a telco supplied DAA was changed by *FCC Rules Part 68* to allow equipment manufacturers to build in their own isolation circuitry as long as it is certified as complaint by the FCC. Like all government certification procedures, the process of getting a design approved can be expensive, time consuming, and tangled in red tape. Only equipment manufacturers should consider such a course—systems integrators, end-user organizations, and amateurs should plan on buying equipment already approved for direct connection. Building a direct-access circuit that will work is easy; building one that complies with all FCC specifications can be difficult.

ECHO SUPPRESSION

Many long-haul telephone circuits are equipped with echo suppressors to prevent a speaker from having to listen to an echo of his own words returned by unavoidable coupling between the remote ends of the receive and transmit paths. Basically a speech detector in the outbound path causes an attenuator to be switched into the inbound path whenever outbound speech is present. This cannot be tolerated in full-duplex data communication. In fact, the slow switching rates of most echo suppressors make them unacceptable for half-duplex data operation as well. Most echo suppressors in North America are designed so that they can be disabled by a control tone sent by the terminating equipment at either or both ends of the connection. Typically a 400 millisecond tone with a frequency falling between 2010 and 2240 Hz will disable most echo suppressors. However, the suppressor will be reenabled if no signal is transmitted from either end for approximately 50 milliseconds.

CHANNEL CAPACITY

In 1949, Shannon showed that the maximum information capacity, C, of a channel contaminated with additive white Gaussian noise is given by:

$$C = W \log_2(1 + S/N)$$

where S is the transmitted signal power and N is the noise power. The value of C given by Shannon's formula represents a theoretical maximum based primarily on information theory considerations; Shannon never provided a practical method for achieving or even approaching this limit in the real world.

In his classic works of 1924 and 1928, Nyquist established a different bound on channel capacity based on constraints that were different from those used by Shannon. In general, the Nyquist limit is lower than the Shannon limit, but it can be achieved by real world systems. Nyquist's development was based on an analysis of ideally bandlimited pulses. Such pulses have time and frequency domain waveforms as shown in Fig. 5-9. Since these pulses are not duration limited, it is easy to see how successive pulses will overlap as in Fig. 5-10 and cause *intersymbol interference*. However, Nyquist showed that intersymbol interference can be avoided if the symbol pulses are transmitted at a rate equal to exactly twice their bandwidth. This will cause the central peak of each pulse to coincide with the zero crossings of all the other pulses as shown in Fig. 5-11. Thus, if the receiver samples the received signal at precisely these points, the amplitude of each symbol's peak can be determined

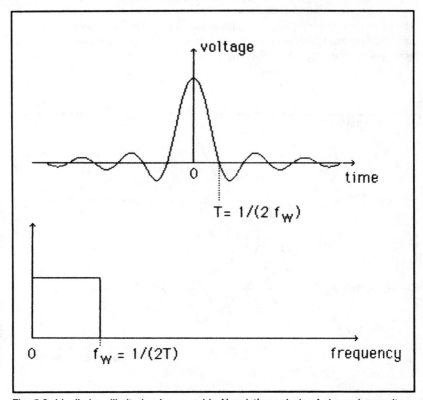

Fig. 5-9. Ideally bandlimited pulses used in Nyquist's analysis of channel capacity.

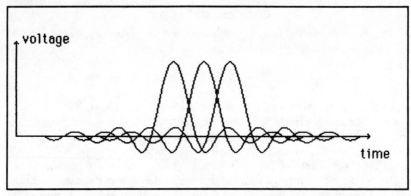

Fig. 5-10. Intersymbol interference caused by overlapping signal pulses.

without interfering contributions from adjacent symbols. The conclusion of Nyquist's analysis is that 2W symbols per second can be transmitted in a signal having a bandwidth of W. "Symbols per second" is often expressed as "bauds." "Bauds" and "bits per second" are equivalent only in the particular case where one symbol represents one bit. In general, the number of bits, n, which can be represented by each symbol is given by:

$$n = \log_2 L$$

where L is the number of distinguishable signals levels. Therefore according to Nyquist, the maximum number of bits per second, C, which can be transmitted through a channel of bandwidth W is given by:

$$C = 2 \, n \, W = 2 \, W \log_2 L.$$

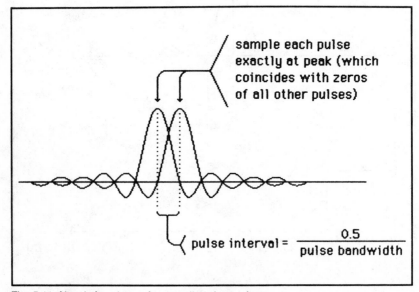

Fig. 5-11. Nyquist's scheme for sampling data pulses.

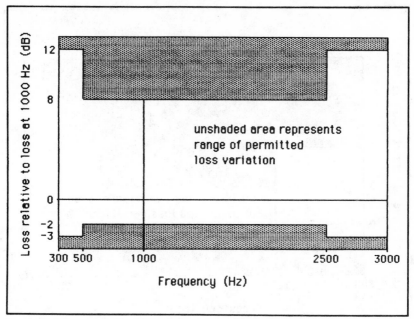

Fig. 5-12. Attenuation distortion characteristic of basic 3002 channel.

The maximum channel capacity indicated by Shannon's formula is never achieved in practice because very complex data encoding and prohibitively expensive modems would be required in order to maintain acceptably low bit error rates. The maximum practical data rate, $S\theta$, currently achievable over telephone lines can be estimated by:

$$S\theta = W (0.09 R_{SN} + 0.75)$$

where W is the bandwidth in Hertz, and
   R_{SN} is the signal-to-noise ratio in dB.

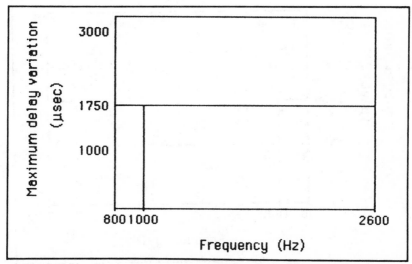

Fig. 5-13. Envelope delay distortion characteristic of basic 3002 channel.

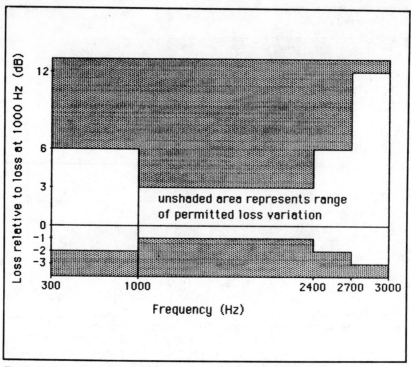

Fig. 5-14. Attenuation distortion characteristic of C1 conditioned lines.

LINE CONDITIONING

As we will see in Chapter 6, the worst case noise and distortion characteristics of some telco lines may be too poor for successful operation of certain types of data

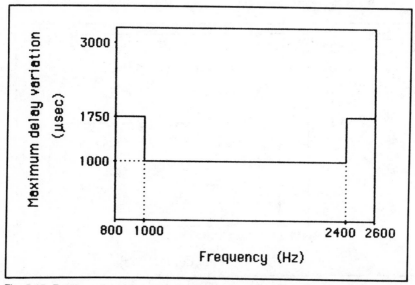

Fig. 5-15. Envelope delay distortion characteristic of C1 conditioned lines.

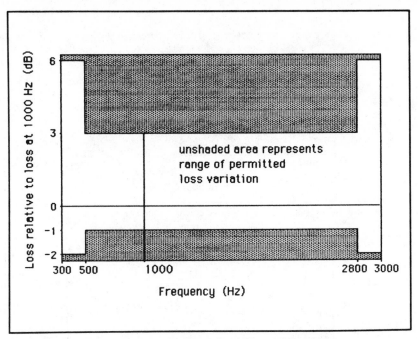

Fig. 5-16. Attenuation distortion characteristic of C2 conditioned lines.

modems. When leasing lines it is possible to obtain *conditioned lines* that exhibit more favorable characteristics for datacomm applications. A range of *Type C* conditioning is available for improved attenuation distortion and envelope delay distortion characteristics. The worst-case limits for basic service and conditioning types C1 through C5 are shown in Figs. 5-12 through 5-25.

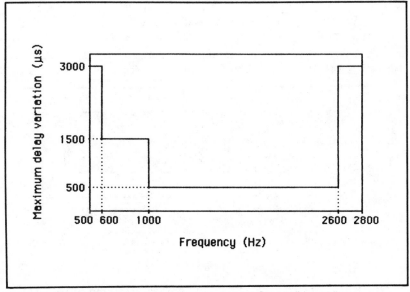

Fig. 5-17. Envelope delay distortion characteristic of C2 conditioned lines.

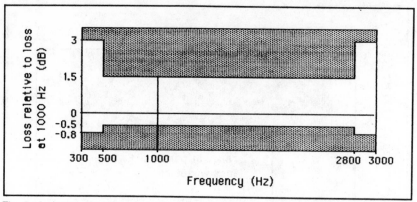

Fig. 5-18. Attenuation distortion characteristic of C3 conditioned access lines.

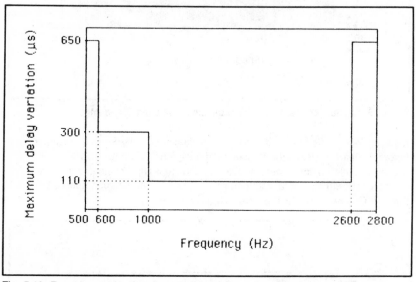

Fig. 5-19. Envelope delay distortion characteristic of C3 conditioned access lines.

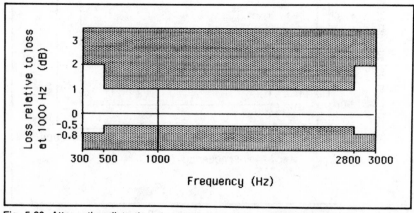

Fig. 5-20. Attenuation distortion characteristic of C3 conditioned trunks.

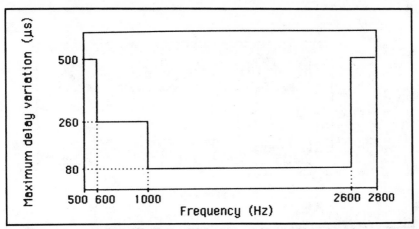

Fig. 5-21. Envelope delay distortion characteristic of C3 conditioned trunks.

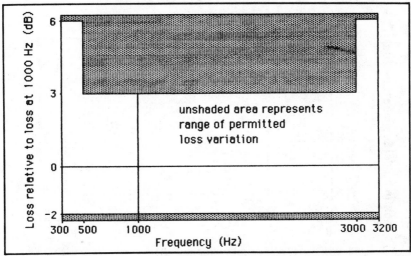

Fig. 5-22. Attenuation distortion characteristic of C4 conditioned lines.

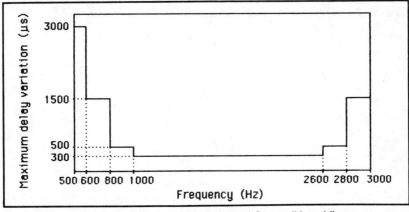

Fig. 5-23. Envelope delay distortion characteristic of C4 conditioned lines.

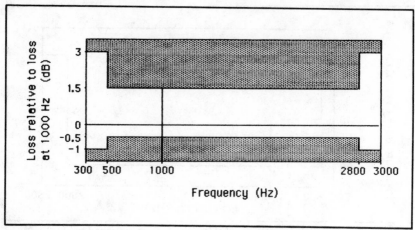

Fig. 5-24. Attenuation distortion characteristic of C5 conditioned lines.

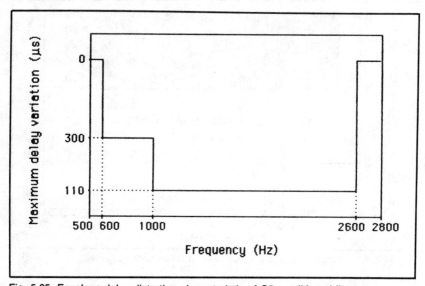

Fig. 5-25. Envelope delay distortion characteristic of C5 conditioned lines.

Chapter 6

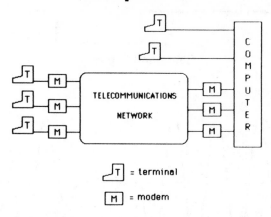

[T] = terminal

[M] = modem

Modulator Carrier Transmission of Digital Data

I N CHAPTER 5 WE SAW HOW THE FREQUENCY RESPONSE OF TRUNKS AND LOCAL loops in the public telephone networks are often somewhat restrictive for data communication. Although transmission of certain baseband data signals can be accommodated by these responses, the signals will generally have to be converted into another form for efficient and reliable transmission. This conversion usually involves three basic modulation techniques—*amplitude modulation, frequency modulation,* or *phase modulation*—used alone or in combinations with each other. These three modulation types are illustrated in Fig. 6-1. FM and PM are very similar and they are often lumped together as *angle modulation.*

AMPLITUDE MODULATION

In amplitude modulation, or AM, the amplitude of a constant-frequency sinusoidal carrier is varied as a function of the baseband signal. This is equivalent to multiplying the carrier by an appropriately scaled version of the baseboard data. Depending upon the scaling of the modulation peak relative to the carrier peak, the resulting signal can vary as shown in Fig. 6-2. The ratio of peak modulation amplitude to peak carrier amplitude is the *modulation index.* In cases where the modulation function can take on only a few discrete values, amplitude modulation is usually referred to as *amplitude-shift keying* or *ASK.* Amplitude modulation with a binary-valued modulation function (i.e. a serial digital data stream) and a modulation index of one, is equivalent to switching the carrier off and on in a pattern that corresponds to the sequence of data bits. This is called *on-off keying* or *OOK.* The frequency spectrum of an AM signal consists of two frequency-shifted copies of the baseband spectrum combined with the carrier spectrum as shown in Fig. 6-3. Since there is copy of the

65

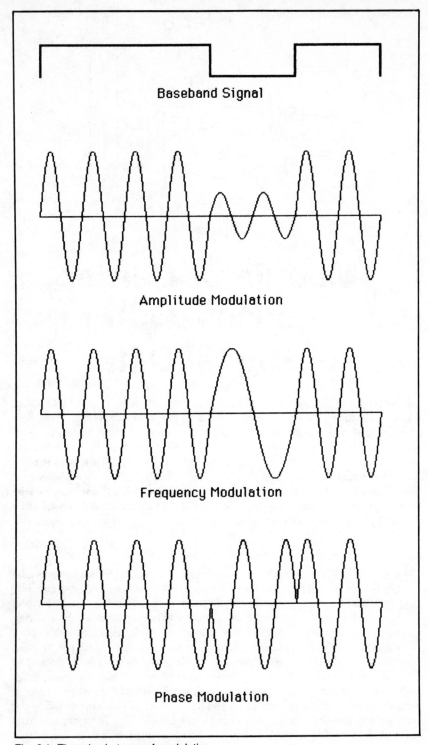

Baseband Signal

Amplitude Modulation

Frequency Modulation

Phase Modulation

Fig. 6-1. Three basic types of modulation.

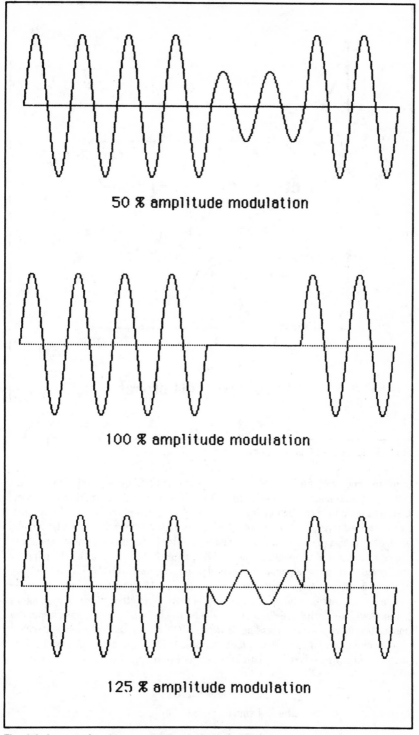

50 % amplitude modulation

100 % amplitude modulation

125 % amplitude modulation

Fig. 6-2. Impact of various modulation indices in AM.

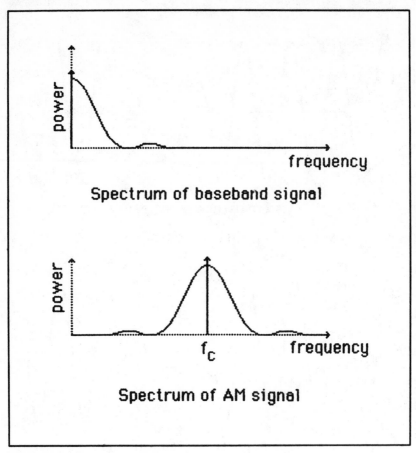

Fig. 6-3. Spectrum of an AM signal.

baseband spectrum both above and below the carrier frequency, this form of AM is referred to as *double sideband* (DSB). A number of useful variations on the basic DSB-AM technique can be obtained by eliminating some of the redundant information contained in the DSB spectrum. Either one of the sidebands can be eliminated (either by filtering or by modulation techniques that generate only one sideband) as shown in Fig. 6-4 to form *single sideband AM* (SSB-AM). If one of the sidebands is greatly reduced but not eliminated, the result is *vestigial sideband AM* (VSB-AM) shown in Fig. 6-5. Since a large part of the energy in an AM signal occurs at the carrier frequency, the carrier is often suppressed to achieve more efficient use of transmitter power. As better techniques become available, the use of AM for data communication via telephone lines is decreasing. However, OOK remains an important and widely used technique for transmission of data via radio links—especially when used in conjunction with Morse code by both amateur and commercial radio operators.

ANGLE MODULATION

In general, an angle-modulated signal can be represented as

$$x(t) = A \cos(\omega_c t + \phi(t))$$

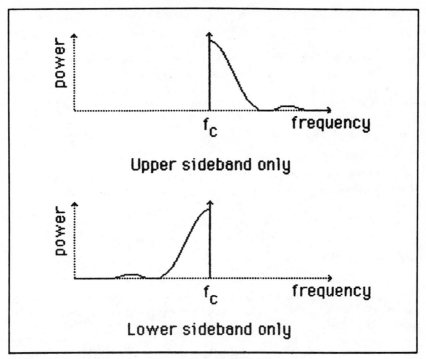

Fig. 6-4. Frequency spectra of single sideband AM signals.

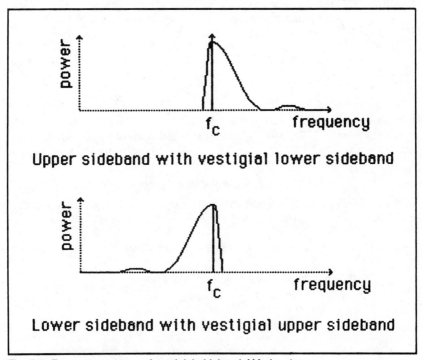

Fig. 6-5. Frequency spectra of vestigial sideband AM signals.

where x(t) is the instantaneous amplitude of the modulated signal at time t

    A is the peak carrier amplitude

    ω_c is the carrier frequency in radians per second,and

    $\phi(t)$ is the angle modulation in radians. (For data transmission applications, $\phi(t)$ will be a function of the baseboard data signal to be transmitted.)

The *instantaneous phase* of such a signal is defined as the total argument of the cosine function, i.e.,

$$\phi_{inst} = \omega_c + \phi(t)$$

where $\phi(t)$ defines the *instantaneous phase deviation*

The *instantaneous frequency* is defined as the first derivative of the instantaneous phase:

$$\omega_{inst} = \frac{d}{dt} \quad [\omega_c t + \phi(t)]$$
$$= \quad \omega_c + \phi'(t)$$

The first derivative of the instantaneous phase defines the *instantaneous frequency deviation*. If the instantaneous phase deviation is made to be proportional to the modulating signal, i.e.,

$$\phi(t) = K\, m(t)$$

then the result is called *phase modulation* (PM). If the modulating signal is a train of rectangular pulses representing digital data, PM is more specifically called *phase-shift keying*(PSK). If the instantaneous frequency deviation is made to be proportional to the modulating signal, i.e.,

$$\phi'(t) = K\, m(t) \quad \text{or}$$
$$\phi(t) = K \int m(t)\, dt,$$

then the result is called *frequency modulation* (FM). If m(t) is a train of rectangular pulses representing digital data, FM is more specifically called *frequency-shift keying* (FSK).

FREQUENCY-SHIFT KEYING

In FSK modulation, the frequency of the carrier is varied as a function of the modulating data. The *modulation index*, m, for an FSK signal is defined as:

$$m = T\,(f_s - f_m)$$

where T is the duration of each bit (1/T is the bit rate.)

    f_s is the keyed frequency for space, and

    f_m is the keyed frequency for mark.

    In general, frequency modulation is a nonlinear process, and determination of an FM signal's frequency spectrum is a rather difficult undertaking. However in the case of FSK certain simplifications are introduced that make the problem considerably more manageable. Consider the case where a binary rectangular train of baseband pulses is used to frequency modulate a sinusoidal carrier. The resulting FSK waveform will be equal to the sum of two amplitude-modulated signals as shown in Fig. 6-6. Assuming random baseband data and an integer number of carrier cycles in each

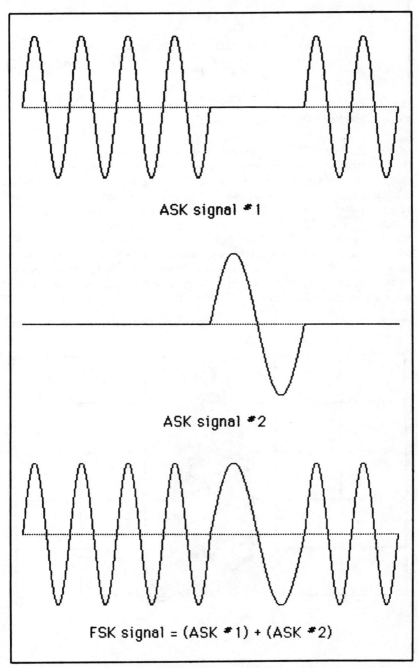

Fig. 6-6. Relationship between FSK and ASK signals.

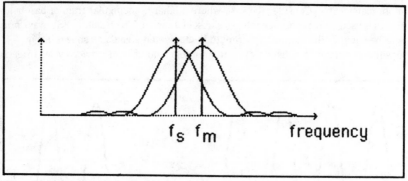

Fig. 6-7. Spectra of ASK signals comprising an FSK signal.

bit interval, these ASK signals will have power spectra as shown in Fig. 6-7. Since the FSK signal is a sum of two ASK signals, its spectrum should be equal to the vector sum of the two ASK signal spectra. Performing such a summation directly is confounded by the fact that the two ASK signals are both random and therefore have only power spectra that do not contain the phase information needed to perform a vector addition. However, the spectrum of an FSK signal can be computed by statistical methods, which are beyond the scope of this book. As shown in Figs. 6-8 through 6-11, the shape of the spectrum will vary for different values of the modulation index, but these shapes are consistent with what we would intuitively expect for the summation of two ASK spectra offset in frequency from each other by different values of the modulation index. Obviously, an FSK modulator designed for

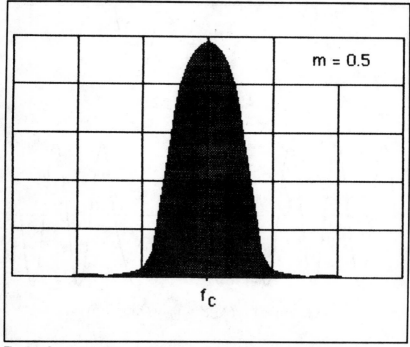

Fig. 6-8. Spectrum of binary FSK signal with modulation index of 0.5.

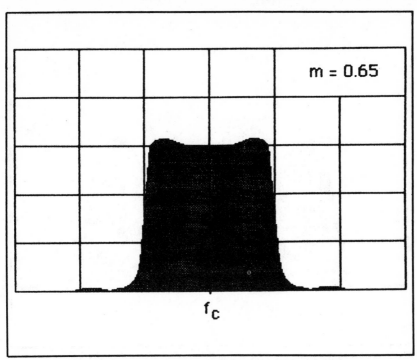

Fig. 6-9. Spectrum of binary FSK signal with modulation index of 0.65.

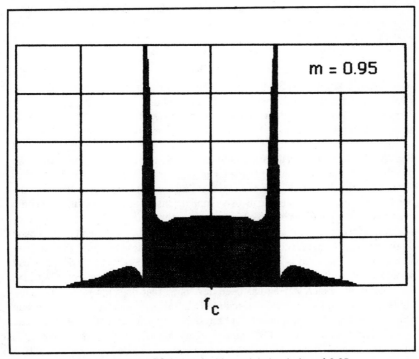

Fig. 6-10. Spectrum of binary FSK signal with modulation index of 0.95.

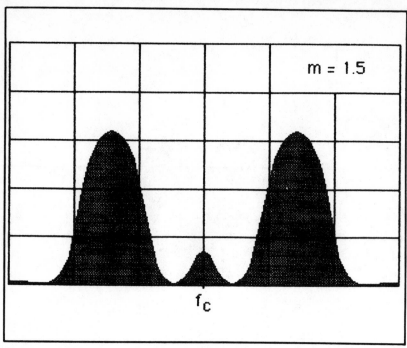

Fig. 6-11. Spectrum of binary FSK signal with modulation index of 1.5.

a particular data rate must use a value for the modulation index that will result in a spectrum that can be accommodated within the bandwidth of the intended transmission channel.

PHASE MODULATION

In phase-shift keying or PSK the phase of a constant-frequency sinusoidal carrier is varied as a function of the sequence of baseband data bits. For binary PSK, the carrier phase is typically shifted by $+90°$ for a mark and by $-90°$ for a space as shown in Fig. 6-12. Since it can be cumbersome to draw out the waveforms for more complicated PSK schemes the vector notation of Fig. 6-13 is usually used in lieu of Fig. 6-12. To derive the maximum benefit from PSK, schemes having more than two possible phase shifts are usually needed. One popular arrangement provides for four different phase shifts with each one representing one of the four possible combinations of two bits, as shown in Fig. 6-14. A similar scheme using eight different shifts to represent combinations of three bits is also possible. Since a PSK signal will contain only *relative* phase information, recovery of the baseboard data bits will depend on the availability of an accurate reference of known phase to which the received signal can be compared in order to establish absolute phase. In practice, this can sometimes be a difficult thing to accomplish. Therefore a modified type of PSK called differential phase-shift keying has been developed that does not require absolute phase information for successful decoding. In DPSK the value of each bit or group of bits is contained in the amount of phase shift from one symbol to the next. The physical characteristics of a DPSK signal are indistinguishable from an ordinary PSK signal, the only difference lies in how the data bits are encoded into the transmitted signal.

74

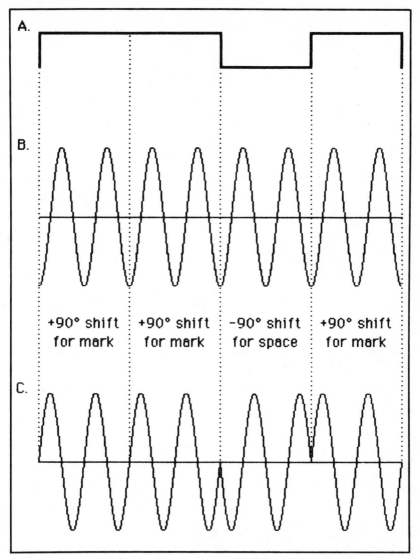

Fig. 6-12. Binary phase-shift keying. (A. Baseband signal. B. Carrier signal. C. Phase-shift keyed signal.)

When typical analog modulating signals are used, the time domain waveforms and spectra of FM and PM signals will generally appear very similar. However, when digital modulating signals are involved, the spectrum of a PSK signal can be made more like the spectrum of an ASK signal. If binary rectangular pulses are used to coherently phase modulate a sinusoidal carrier, the resulting PSK signal can be represented as the sum of an ASK signal and an inverted copy of its carrier as shown in Fig. 6-15. Thus, a rectangular-pulse PSK signal is also a suppressed-carrier ASK signal and it will exhibit a power spectrum as shown in Fig. 6-16. The zero points of this spectrum occur at the carrier frequency plus or minus integer multiplies of the baud rate.

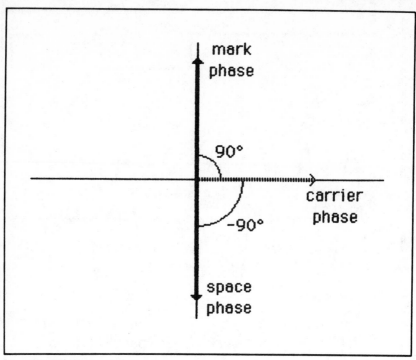

Fig. 6-13. PSK vector notation.

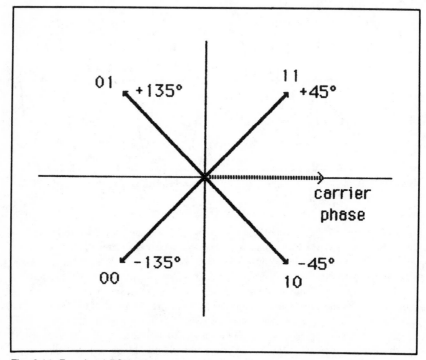

Fig. 6-14. Four level PSK scheme.

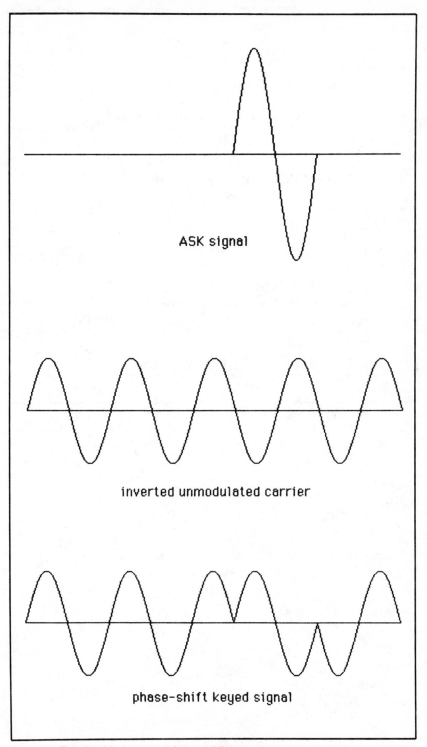

ASK signal

inverted unmodulated carrier

phase-shift keyed signal

Fig. 6-15. Relationship between ASK and PSK signals.

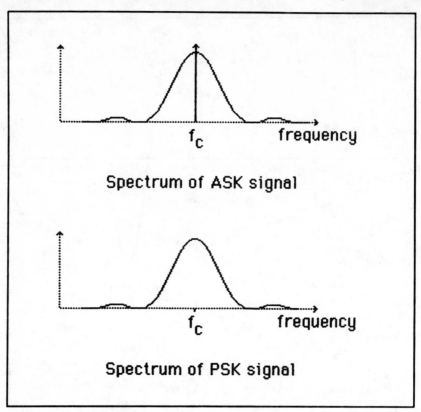

Fig. 6-16. Similarity between ASK and PSK spectra.

Chapter 7

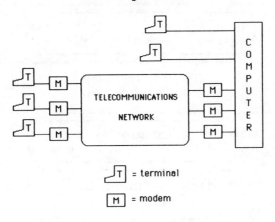

$\boxed{\underset{T}{\rule{0pt}{0pt}}}$ = terminal

$\boxed{M}$ = modem

RS-232-C

T HE ELECTRONIC INDUSTRIES ASSOCIATION HAS FORMULATED THE RS-232 STAN-
dards in an attempt to standardize the interface between modems and the data
terminal equipment connected to them. The latest version, *RS-232C—Interface Between Data Terminal Equipment and Data Communication Equipment Employed Binary
Data Interchange,* was adopted in 1969. Although it was originally intended to specify
the interface between a terminal ("data terminal equipment") and a modem ("data
communication equipment"), RS-232C has become widespread throughout the computer industry as a definition of the serial interface between computers and their
peripheral equipment. Of course, in many of these applications only parts of the standard are implemented, and often these implementations are only partially compliant
with the standard specifications.

CIRCUITS IN THE INTERFACE

The standard calls for a cable equipped with 25-pin connectors to be used for interfacing the terminal and modem. Although the standard does not specify what type
of connector to use, the DB-25 twenty-five pin 'D' connector shown in Fig. 7-1 has
become the de facto standard throughout the industry. The standard, however, *does*
specify the assignment of specific interface circuits to specific connector pins as shown
in Table 7-1.

GROUNDS

Circuit AA, *protective ground,* is connected to the protective ground of the terminal
equipment. This circuit is included only for safety reasons, and it is not involved in

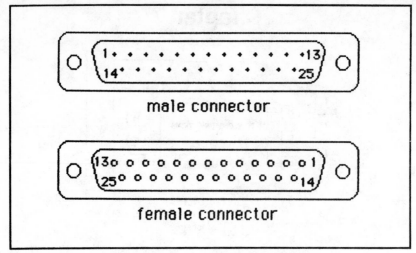

Fig. 7-1. DB-25 connector usually used in RS-232-C interfaces.

any signaling through the interface. Circuit AB, *signal ground,* serves as the ground reference for all of the other signals in the interface.

DATA CIRCUITS

Circuit BA, *transmit data,* carries the outbound data signal from the terminal, where it is generated, to the modem for subsequent modulation and long-haul transmission. The terminal should send data to the modem only while the signals on circuits CA, CB, CC, and CD are all asserted. When not sending data, the terminal should hold circuit BA in a constant MARK state.

Circuit BB, *receive data,* carries the inbound data signal from the modem, where it is demodulated from the long-haul reception, to the terminal. This circuit should be held in a constant marking state whenever the signal on circuit CF is not asserted.

TIMING CIRCUITS

For synchronous transmission, the transmit data on circuit BA can be clocked in one or two different ways. The terminal can provide a clock signal to the modem via circuit DA, *transmitter signal element timing (DTE source),* or the modem can issue a demand clock to the terminal via circuit Db, *transmitter signal element timing (DCE source).* In the clock provided by the terminal, the ON to OFF transitions concide with the nominal center of each data bit on circuit BA as shown in Fig. 7-2. When responding to the demand clock present on the circuit DB, the terminal will provide data on circuit BA such that the transitions between bits will nominally coincide with the OFF to ON transitions of the demand clock as shown in Fig. 7-3.

In synchronous installations, circuit DD, *receiver signal element timing (DCE source),* carries a receive-data clock signal from the modem to the terminal. The ON to OFF transitions of the clock coincide with the nominal center of each data bit on circuit BB, *receive data.*

CONTROL CIRCUITS

Circuit CA, *request to send,* carries a control signal from the terminal to the modem.

Whenever this signal is asserted the modem will operate in the transmit mode, and whenever the signal is not asserted the modem will operate in the receive mode. Half-duplex operation is achieved through appropriate control of this signal. When CA is switched from OFF to ON, the modem will enter the transmit mode and indicate its readiness to accept transmit data from the terminal by asserting circuit CB (clear to send). When CA is switched from ON to OFF, the modem will de-assert CA and enter the receive mode.

Circuit CB, *clear to send*, carries a control signal from the modem to the terminal. The signal on this circuit is assorted whenever the modem is in the transmit mode

Table 7-1. RS-232-C Connector Pin Assignments.

pin	symb.	signal description	signal source
1	AA	protective ground	
2	BA	transmit data	term.
3	BB	receive data	modem
4	CA	request to send	term.
5	CB	clear to send	modem
6	CC	data set ready	modem
7	AB	signal ground	
8	CF	rec. line signal det.	modem
9		reserved	
10		reserved	
11		unassigned	
12	SCF	sec. rec. line sig. det.	modem
13	SCB	sec. clear to send	modem
14	SBA	sec. transmit data	term.
15	DB	transm. sig. elem. timing	modem
16	SBB	sec. receive data	modem
17	DD	recvr. sig. elem. timing	modem
18		unassigned	
19	SCA	sec. request to send	term.
20	CD	data terminal ready	term.
21	CG	signal quality	modem
22	CE	ring indicator	modem
23	CH;CI	data sig. rate select	t / m
24	DA	transm. sig. elem. timing	term.
25		unassigned	

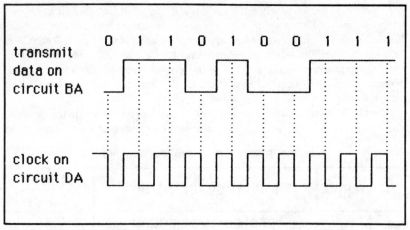

Fig. 7-2. Nominal timing relationship between signals on RS-232-C circuits DA and BA.

and ready to accept transmit data from the terminal. The modem's readiness to accept data from the terminal may be delayed while waiting for the far-end modem to indicate readiness to receive from the long-haul channel.

Circuit CC, *data set ready,* carries a control signal from the modem to the terminal. The signal on this circuit is asserted by the modem after it determines that the long-haul connection to the distant modem has been established and is ready for data use. Whenever this signal is not asserted, the terminal should ignore all other circuits except CE (*ring indicator*).

Circuit CD, *data terminal ready,* carries a control signal from the terminal to the modem. The signal on this circuit is asserted whenever the terminal is ready to communicate through the modem.

Circuit CE, *ring indicator,* carries a control signal from the modem to the terminal. The signal on this circuit is asserted whenever the modem detects a ringing signal on the long-haul channel.

Circuit CF, *received line signal detector,* carries a control signal from the modem to the terminal. The signal on this circuit is asserted whenever the modem determines that it is receiving an appropriate signal from the distant modem via the long-

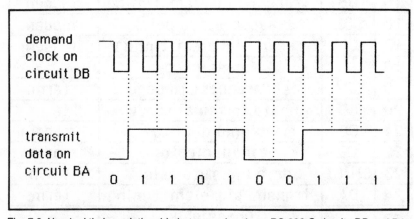

Fig. 7-3. Nominal timing relationship between signals on RS-232-C circuits DB and BA.

haul channel. If the received long-haul signal is lost or unsuitable for demodulation, the modem will de-assert the signal on circuit CF.

Circuit CG, *signal quality detector,* carries a control signal from the modem to the terminal. The signal on this circuit is asserted whenever the modem determines that the received long-haul signal appears to be normal. If the modem determines that the quality of the received signal is marginal and that there is a high probability of error, the signal on CG will be de-asserted.

Circuit CH, *data signal rate selector (DTE source),* carries a control signal from the terminal to the modem. In installations involving dual-rate modems, the signal on this circuit indicates which of the two possible data rates the terminal will be using to send data to the modem. An ON condition indicates that the higher of the two rates will be used.

Circuit CI, *data signal rate selector (DCE source),* carries a control signal from the modem to the terminal. In installations involving dual-rate modems, the signal on this circuit indicates which of the two possible data rates the modem will be using to send data to the terminal. An ON condition indicates that the higher of the two rates will be used.

SECONDARY CIRCUITS

As we will discover in Chapter 9, some modems such as the Bell 202 support a low-speed secondary channel that operates independently from the primary channel. To exploit this feature, the interface to these modems must contain several data and control circuits that operate independently from the primary circuits. Circuit SBA, *secondary transmitted data*, is similar to circuit BA (*transmit data*) except it carries the secondary data signal from the terminal, where it is generated, to the modem for subsequent modulation and long-haul transmission via the secondary channel. The terminal should send secondary data to the modem only while the signals on circuits SCA, SCB, CC and CD are all asserted. Circuit SBB, *secondary received data*, is similar to circuit BB except it carries the secondary demodulated received-data signal from the modem to the terminal. Circuit SCA, *secondary request to send,* and circuit SCB, *secondary clear to send*, serve the same purposes for the secondary channel that CA and CB serve for the primary channel. When the secondary channel is restricted to serving as a backward channel in half-duplex installations, measures must be implemented to insure that the secondary channel is enabled to transmit only when the primary is receiving. The signal on circuit SCF, *secondary received line signal detector*, is asserted whenever the modem determines that it is receiving an appropriate secondary signal from the distant modem via the long-haul channel. If the received long-haul secondary signal disappears or becomes unsuitable for demodulation, the modem will de-assert the signal on circuit SCF.

CONFIGURATION OPTIONS

All of the circuits described need not be included in every RS-232C interface. In fact, the standard specifies 13 different configurations that are suitable for a variety of common applications. These interface types and the circuits they contain are summarized in Table 7-2. An additional configuration—interface type Z—allows complete freedom to include any particular set of circuits that may be required to support a special application. Note that circuit AA, *protective ground,* is optional in all interface types. Also, circuits CG, CH, and CI are not included in any of the standard interface types but they may be required in special interfaces designed to support high speed modems operating over marginally suitable communications links.

Table 7-2. Circuits Contained in Standard RS-232-C Interface Types.

x-basic circuits y-circ. for synch. oper. z-circ for swit. serv.		AB	BA	BB	CA	CB	CC	CD	CE	CF	DA/DB	DD	SBA	SBB	SCA	SCB	SCF
A	transmit only x	x	x			x	x	z	z		y						
B	transmit only x	x	x		x	x	x	z	z		y						
C	receive only	x		x			x	z	z	x		y					
D	half or full duplex	x	x	x	x	x	x	z	z	x	y	y					
E	duplex	x	x	x		x	x	z	z	x	y	y					
F	pri. chan Rx only sec. chan Tx only	x		x			x	z	z	x		y	x				x
G	pri. chan Tx only sec. chan Rx only	x	x		x	x	x	z	z		y		x		x	x	
H	pri. chan Rx only sec. chan Tx only	x		x			x	z	z	x		y	x				x
I	pri. chan Tx only sec. chan Rx only	x	x		x	x	x	z	z		y		x		x		
J	pri. chan Tx only half duplex sec.	x	x		x	x	x	z	z		y		x	x	x	x	x
K	pri. chan Rx only half duplex sec.	x		x			x	z	z	x	y	y	x	x	x	x	x
L	half or full duplex pri. & sec. chans	x	x	x	x	x	x	z	z	x	y	y	x	x	x	x	x
M	full duplex pri. full duplex sec.	x	x	x		x	x	z	z	x	y	y	x	x		x	x

ELECTRICAL CHARACTERISTICS

The various circuits in the interface are implemented using an *unbalanced* data transmission scheme that was discussed in general terms in Chapter 3. The open-circuit signal voltages can range from -25 V to $+25$ V measured with respect to signal ground (circuit AB). When a load resistance between 3 KΩ and 7 KΩ is applied, the allowable signal range decreases to ± 15 V relative to signal ground. At the receiver, a signal voltage between -3 and -15 V relative to signal ground will be interpreted as MARK for data circuits and as OFF or a de-asserted condition for clock and control circuits. Conversely, a voltage between $+3$ and $+15$ will be interpreted as a SPACE for data circuits and as On or an asserted condition for clock and control circuits. The logical meaning of signals in the transition region between -3 V and $+3$ V is not defined. Signals on all control circuits and on clock and data circuits operating at 40 bps or slower should pass through the transition region in one millisecond or less. Signals on clock and data circuits operating above 40 bps should pass through the transistor region in four percent of a bit time or less. However in no case should the slew rate of the output exceed 20V per microsecond. The standard specifies a maximum data rate of 20 kbps, and 50 feet is the maximum recommended cable length. the driver design should include protective measures that will permit the driver output to withstand an open circuit, or a passive noninductive con-

Table 7-3. Integrated Circuit Drivers for RS-232-C.

Exar	XR1488
Fairchild	9636AC
	75150
	μA1488
Hitachi	HD75188
Motorola	MC1488
National	DS75150
	DS1488
Signetics	SG1488
Silicon General	SG1488
Texas Instruments	MC1488
	SN75188
	SN75150
	μA9636A

nection (including a short) to any other circuit in the interface, without suffering damage itself or causing damage to its associated equipment.

IMPLEMENTATION

Despite all the specifications that must be met, implementation of an RS-232-C interface is really quite simple—thanks to the selection of integrated circuit interface drivers and receivers that are readily available. Tables 7-3 and 7-4 list some drivers and receivers that are RS-232-C compatible.

85

Table 7-4. Integrated Circuit Receivers for RS-232-C.

Fairchild	9617C
	9637AC
	µA1489
	75154
Hitachi	HD75154
Motorola	MC1489
National	DS1489
	DS75154
Signetics	MC1489
Silicon General	SG1489
	SG75154
Texas Instruments	SN75154
	SN75157
	SN75189
	µA9637AC

Chapter 8

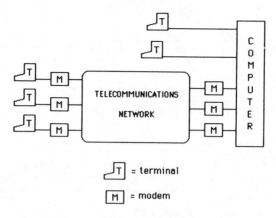

$\boxed{\underline{\text{T}}}$ = terminal

$\boxed{\text{M}}$ = modem

RS-449,
RS-422-A, and RS-423-A

O VER THE YEARS THAT RS-232-C HAS BEEN IN USE, A NUMBER OF SHORTCOM-
ings have become evident. Some of these, such as the limited data rate, excessive RFI, and crosstalk problems require changes so fundamental that an entirely
new set of standards has had to be developed. This set comprises *RS-449, RS-422-A,*
and *RS-423-A.* Electrical characteristics are specified in *RS-422-A—Electrical
Characteristics of Balanced Voltage Digital Interface Circuits* and *RS-423-A—Electrical
Characteristics of Unbalanced Voltage Interface Circuits.* Mechanical and functional
characteristics are specified in *RS-449—General Purpose 37-Position and 9-Position
Interface for Data Terminal Equipment and Data Circuit-Terminating Equipment Employing Serial Binary Data Interchange.*

CIRCUITS AND CONNECTORS

RS-449 calls for a cable equipped with 37-pin connectors to be used for interfacing
the terminal and modem. Furthermore an additional cable with 9-pin connectors is
specified for installations which implement a secondary channel interface. Unlike
RS-232, RS-449 <u>does</u> specify the type of connector to be used. The standard calls
for connectors that meet the intermating dimensions specified in MIL-C-24308. In
English this means that most brands of the DB-9 and DB-37 connectors depicted in
Fig. 8-1 will be acceptable. The connector attached to the modem must have female
contacts and a male shell. The cable that mates with this connector must measure
less than 200 feet from the modem connector up to the terminal equipment. The pin
assignments for primary circuits are listed in Table 8-1, and those for secondary circuits are listed in Table 8-2. Unlike RS-232-C, which specifies identical electrical
characteristics for all signals, RS-449 separates the various circuits into two categor-

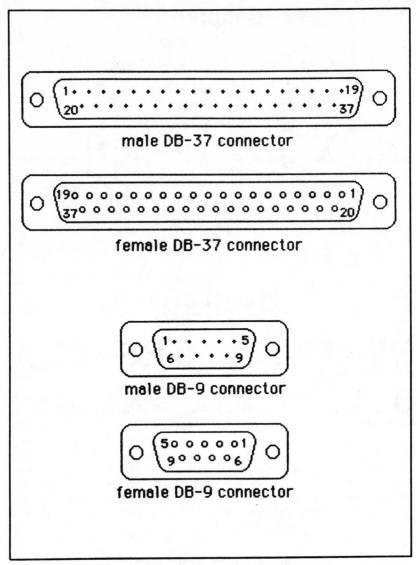

male DB-37 connector

female DB-37 connector

male DB-9 connector

female DB-9 connector

Fig. 8-1. DB-37 and DB-9 connectors used in RS-449 interfaces.

ies and specifies a different set of electrical characteristics for the signals of each category. The category assignments of the circuits are also listed in Tables 8-1 and 8-2.

COMMON CIRCUITS

Circuit SG, *signal ground,* connects together the signal grounds of the terminal and modem. Circuit SC, *send common,* is connected to the signal ground of the terminal and is used as the ground reference for all Category II unbalanced receivers in the modem. In a similar fashion, circuit RC, *receive common,* is connected to the signal ground of the modem and used as a ground reference for all Category II unbalanced receivers in the terminal.

Table 8-1. RS-449 Primary Connector Assignments.

pin	symb.	signal description	cat.	signal source
1		shield		
2	SI	sig. rate indic.	II	modem
3		spare		
4	SD+	send data	I	term.
5	ST+	send timing	I	modem
6	RD+	receive data	I	modem
7	RS+	request to send	I	term.
8	RT+	receive timing	I	modem
9	CS+	clear to send	I	modem
10	LL	local loopback	II	term.
11	DM+	data mode	I	modem
12	TR+	terminal ready	I	term.
13	RR+	receiver ready	I	modem
14	RL	remote loopback	II	term.
15	IC	incoming call	II	modem
16	SF/SR	sel.freq./sig.rate sel.	II	term.
17	TT+	terminal timing	I	term.
18	TM	test mode	II	modem
19	SG	signal ground		term.
20	RC	receive common	II	modem
21		spare		
22	SD-	send data	I	term.
23	ST-	send timing	I	modem
24	RD-	receive data	I	modem
25	RS-	request to send	I	term.
26	RT-	receive timing	I	modem
27	CS-	clear to send	I	modem
28	IS	term. in service	II	term.
29	DM-	data mode	I	modem
30	TR-	terminal ready	I	term.
31	RR-	receiver ready	I	modem
32	SS	select standby	II	term.
33	SQ	signal quality	II	modem
34	NS	new signal	II	term.
35	TT-	terminal timing	I	term.
36	SB	standby indic.	II	modem
37	SC	send common		term.

Table 8-2. RS-449 Secondary Connector Assignments.

pin	symb.	signal description	cat.	signal source
1		shield		
2	SRR	sec. receiver ready	II	modem
3	SSD	sec. send data	II	term.
4	SRD	sec. receive data	II	modem
5	SG	signal ground	II	term.
6	RC	receive common	II	modem
7	SRS	sec. request to send	II	term.
8	SCS	sec. clear to send	II	modem
9	SC	send common	II	term.

DATA CIRCUITS

Circuit SD, *send data*, carries the outbound data signal from the terminal, where it generated, to the modem for subsequent modulation and long-haul transmission. The terminal should send data to the modem only while the signals on circuits RS (*request to send*), CS (*clear to send*), DM (*data mode*), TR (*terminal ready*), and IS (*terminal in service*) are all asserted. When not sending data, the terminal should hold circuit SD in a constant marking condition.

Circuit RD, *receive data*, carries the inbound data signal from the modem, where it is demodulated from the long-haul reception, to the terminal. This circuit should be held in a constant marking state whenever the signal on circuit RR (*receiver ready*) is not asserted.

TIMING CIRCUITS

For synchronous transmission, the transmit data on circuit SD (*send data*) can be clocked in one of two different ways. The terminal can provide a clock signal to the modem via circuit TT, *terminal timing*, or the modem can issue a demand clock to the terminal via circuit ST, *send timing*. In the clock provided by the terminal, the ON to OFF transitions coincide with the nominal center of each data bit on circuit SD as shown in Fig. 8-2. When responding to the demand clock present on circuit ST, the terminal will provide data on circuit SD such that the transitions between bits will nominally coincide with the OFF to ON transitions of the demand clock as shown in Fig. 8-3.

In synchronous installations, circuit RT, *receive timing*, carries a receive-data clock signal from the modem to the terminal. The ON to OFF transitions of the clock coincide with the nominal center of each data bit on circuit RD (*receive data*).

CONTROL CIRCUITS

Circuit RS, *request to send*, carries a control signal from the terminal to the modem. Whenever this signal is asserted the modem will operate in the transmit mode, and whenever the signal is not asserted the modem will operate in the receive mode. Half-duplex operation is achieved through appropriate control of this signal. When RS is switched from OFF to ON, the modem will enter the transmit mode and indicate

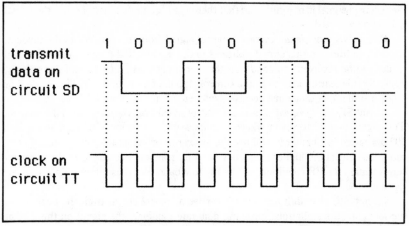

Fig. 8-2. Nominal timing relationship between signals on RS-449 circuits SD and TT.

its readiness to accept transmit data from the terminal by asserting circuit CS (*clear to send*). When RS is switched from ON to OFF, the modem will de-assert CS and enter the receive mode.

Circuit CS, *clear to send,* carries a control signal from the modem to the terminal. The signal on this circuit is asserted whenever the modem is in the transmit mode and ready to accept data from the terminal. The modem's readiness to accept data from the terminal may be delayed while waiting for the far-end modem to indicate readiness to receive from the long-haul channel.

Circuit RR, *receiver ready,* carries a control signal from the modem to the terminal. The signal on this circuit is asserted whenever the modem determines that it is receiving an appropriate signal from the distant modem via the long-haul channel. If the received long-haul signal is lost or unsuitable for demodulation, the modem will de-assert the signal on circuit RR.

Circuit SQ, *signal quality,* carries a control signal from the modem to the terminal. The signal on this circuit is asserted whenever the modem determines that the received long-haul signal appears to be normal. If the modem determines that the quality of

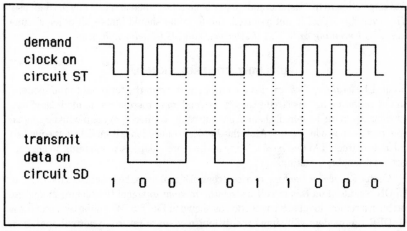

Fig. 8-3. Nominal timing relationship between signals on RS-449 circuits ST and SD.

the received signal is marginal and that there is a high probability of error, the signal will be de-asserted.

Circuit NS, *new signal,* carries a control signal from the terminal to the modem. An ON condition on this circuit indicates to the modem that a new long-haul signal is likely to be received soon and that the modem should prepare itself accordingly. Typically this feature is used at the control station of a multipoint polling system or other installations that must receive switched carrier communications.

Circuit SF, *select frequency,* carries a control signal from the terminal to the modem. This signal is used to select whether an *answer/originate* modem, such as the Bell 103 discussed in Chapter 9, will use the answer or originate frequency sets. An ON condition selects the higher frequency band for transmit and the lower band for receive, while an OFF condition selects the low band for transmit and high band for receive.

Circuit SR, *signaling rate selector,* carries a control signal from the terminal to the modem. In installations involving dual-rate modems, the signal on this circuit indicates which of the two possible data rates the terminal will be using to send data to the modem. An ON condition indicates that the higher of the two rates will be used.

Circuit SI, *signaling rate indicator,* carries a control signal from the modem to the terminal. In installations involving dual-rate modems, the signal on this circuit indicates which of the two possible data rates the modem will be using to send data to the terminal. An ON condition indicates that the higher of the two rates will be used.

Circuit IS, *terminal in service,* carries a control signal from the terminal to the modem. An OFF condition on this circuit indicates to the modem that the terminal is not available for service. Based on this information, the modem can then refuse incoming calls or cause itself to appear busy to a line hunting device attempting to place an incoming call.

Circuit IC, *incoming call,* carries a control signal from the modem to the terminal. The signal on this circuit is asserted whenever the modem detects a ringing signal on the long-haul channel.

Circuit TR, *terminal ready,* carries a control signal from the terminal to the modem. The signal on this circuit is asserted whenever the terminal is ready to communicate through the modem.

Circuit DM, data mode, carries a control signal from the modem to the terminal. The signal on this circuit is asserted by the modem after it determines that the long-haul connection to the distant modem has been established and is ready for data use. Whenever this signal is not asserted, the terminal should ignore all other circuits except IC (*incoming call*), TM (*test mode*), and SB (*standby indicator*).

AUXILIARY CONTROL SIGNALS

Circuit LL, *local loopback,* carries a control signal from the terminal to the modem. An ON condition on this circuit causes the modem to disconnect its modulated output signal from the long-haul channel and internally connect it to the modulated signal input port as shown in Fig. 8-4. After this *loopback* connection is established, the modem will assert circuit TM (*test mode*). Many of the more inexpensive modems do not support local loopback testing.

Circuit RL, *remote loopback,* carries a control signal from the terminal to the modem. An ON condition on this circuit causes the modem to signal the distant modem to establish a remote loopback connection as shown in Fig. 8-5. When the terminal turns RL OFF, the modem will signal the distant modem to return to normal operation. Many of the more inexpensive modems do not support remote loopback testing, and

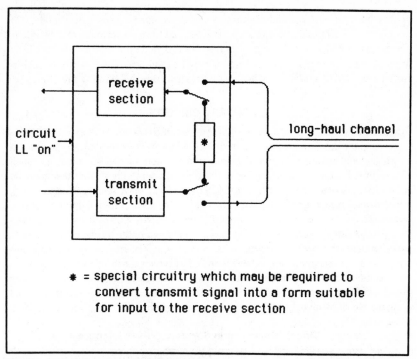

circuit
LL "on"

long-haul channel

* = special circuitry which may be required to
convert transmit signal into a form suitable
for input to the receive section

Fig. 8-4. RS-449 local loopback test connections.

many modem standards are inherently unable to support the modem-to-modem signaling needed to implement this function.

Circuit TM, *test mode*, carries a control signal from the modem to the terminal. The modem asserts this circuit to indicate that it is operating in a test mode itself

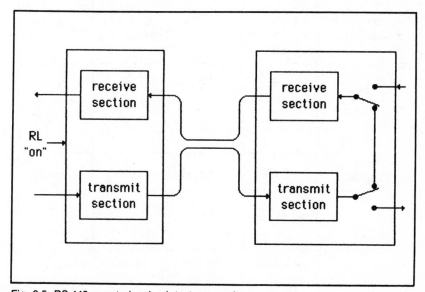

RL
"on"

Fig. 8-5. RS-449 remote loopback test connections.

or that the long-haul communications facilities are operating in a test mode.

Circuit SS, *select standby,* carries a control signal from the terminal to the modem. The terminal will assert this circuit to instruct the modem to use standby facilities in place of the normal long-haul communications facilities. The modem will assert circuit SB, *standby indicator,* whenever it is set to use the standby facilities.

SECONDARY CIRCUITS

Circuit SSD, *secondary send data,* is similar to circuit SD (send data) except it carries the secondary data signal from the terminal, where it is generated, to the modem for subsequent modulation and long-haul transmission via the secondary channel. The terminal should send secondary data to the modem only while the signals on circuits SRS (*secondary request to send*), SCS (*secondary clear to send*), DM (*data mode*), TR *(terminal ready),* and IS (*terminal in service*) are all asserted. Circuit SRD, *secondary receive data,* is similar to circuit RD (*receive date*) except it carries the secondary demodulated received-data signal from the modem to the terminal. Circuit SRS, *secondary request to send,* and circuit SCS, *secondary clear to send,* serve the same purposes for the secondary channel that RS and CS serve for the primary channel. When the secondary channel is restricted to serving as a backward channel in half-duplex installations, measures must be implemented to insure that the secondary channel is enabled to transmit only when the primary is receiving. The signal on circuit SRR,

Table 8-3. Circuits Contained in Standard RS-449 Interface Types.

	Configuration type			
	Send & Receive (SR)	Send Only (SO)	Receive Only (RO)	Data & Timing Only (DT)
Mandatory circuits	SG, SC, RC DM, SD, RD RS, CS, RR TM	SG, SC, RC DM, SD, RS CS, TM	SG, SC, RS DM, RR, TM	SG, SD, RD
Circ. req. for switched serv.	TR	TR	TR	
Circ. req. for switched serv. with ans. signal	IC	IC	IC	
Circ. req. for synch. operation	ST, RT	ST	RT	ST, RT
Optional circuits	TT, IS, SQ NS, SF, SR SI, SSD SRD, SRS SCS, SRR LL, RL SS, SB	IS, TT, SF SR, SI, SSD SRD, SRS SCS, SRR SS, SB	IS, SQ, NS SF, SR, SI SSD, SRD SRS, SCS SRR, SS, SB	TT

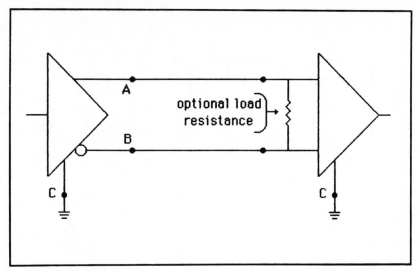

Fig. 8-6. RS-442-A balanced interface circuit.

secondary received line signal detector, is asserted whenever the modem determines that it is receiving an appropriate secondary signal from the distant modem via the long-haul channel. If the received long-haul secondary signal disappears or becomes unsuitable for demodulation, the modem will de-assert the signal on circuit SRR.

CONFIGURATION OPTIONS

RS-449 specifies four different standard interfaces—*Type SR* (send and receive), *Type SO* (send only), *Type RO* (receive only), and *Type DT* (data and timing only). The circuits contained in each configuration are summarized in Table 8-3.

ELECTRICAL CHARACTERISTICS

Category I circuits (see Table 8-1 for categories of specific circuits) operating at data rates of 20 kbps or less can use either the balanced electrical characteristics of RS-422-A or the unbalanced electrical characteristics of RS-423-A. As shown in Fig. 8-6, the specifications in RS-422-A include an optional termination resistance that should not be used in this situation. Category I circuits operating at data rates in excess of 20 kbps must use the balanced electrical characteristics of RS-422-A with use of the terminating resistor optional. At all data rates, Category II circuits must use the unbalanced electrical characteristics of RS-423-A. This unbalanced interface employs a balanced receiver that is identical to the receiver used in the balanced RS-422-A configuration.

Unlike unbalanced drivers in which signal voltages are measured with respect to ground, the signal voltages of an RS-422-A balanced driver are measured between the A and B outputs of the driver. Conditions where A is negative with respect to B are interpreted as MARK for data circuits and as OFF or a de-asserted condition for clock and control circuits. Conversely, conditions where B is negative with respect to A are interpreted as SPACE for data circuits and as ON or an asserted condition for clock and control circuits. The driver electrical parameters and their measurement points are depicted in Figs. 8-7 through 8-10, and transient performance specifications are illustrated in Fig. 8-11. When voltages from minus ten to plus ten are applied

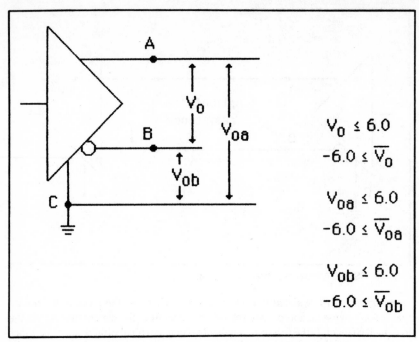

$$V_0 \leq 6.0$$
$$-6.0 \leq \overline{V_0}$$

$$V_{0a} \leq 6.0$$
$$-6.0 \leq \overline{V_{0a}}$$

$$V_{0b} \leq 6.0$$
$$-6.0 \leq \overline{V_{0b}}$$

Fig. 8-7. Open-circuit voltage specifications for RS-422-A balanced drivers.

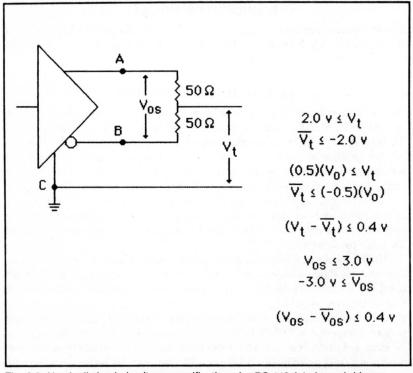

$$2.0 \text{ v} \leq V_t$$
$$\overline{V_t} \leq -2.0 \text{ v}$$

$$(0.5)(V_0) \leq V_t$$
$$\overline{V_t} \leq (-0.5)(V_0)$$

$$(V_t - \overline{V_t}) \leq 0.4 \text{ v}$$

$$V_{0s} \leq 3.0 \text{ v}$$
$$-3.0 \text{ v} \leq \overline{V_{0s}}$$

$$(V_{0s} - \overline{V_{0s}}) \leq 0.4 \text{ v}$$

Fig. 8-8. Nominally-loaded voltage specifications for RS-442-A balanced drivers.

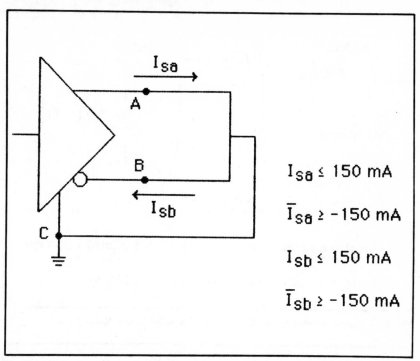

Fig. 8-9. Short-circuit current specification for RS-422-A balanced drivers.

$I_{sa} \le 150 \text{ mA}$

$\overline{I}_{sa} \ge -150 \text{ mA}$

$I_{sb} \le 150 \text{ mA}$

$\overline{I}_{sb} \ge -150 \text{ mA}$

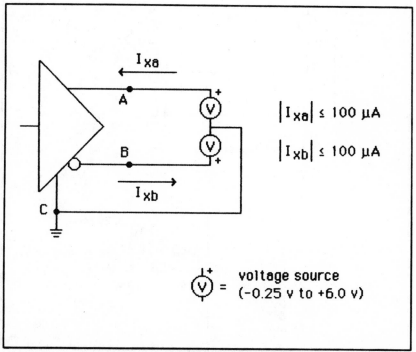

$|I_{xa}| \le 100 \text{ }\mu\text{A}$

$|I_{xb}| \le 100 \text{ }\mu\text{A}$

$\underset{V}{\textcircled{V}} = $ voltage source (-0.25 v to +6.0 v)

Fig. 8-10. Power-off leakage current specifications for RS-422-A balanced drivers.

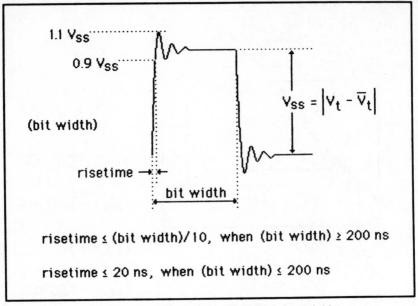

risetime $\leq$ (bit width)/10, when (bit width) $\geq$ 200 ns

risetime $\leq$ 20 ns, when (bit width) $\leq$ 200 ns

Fig. 8-11. Output waveform specifications for RS-422-A balanced drivers.

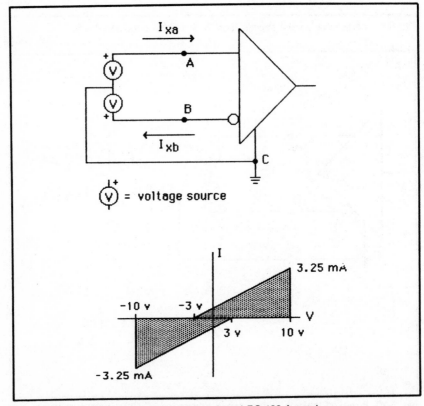

Fig. 8-12. Input characteristics for RS-422-A and RS-423-A receivers.

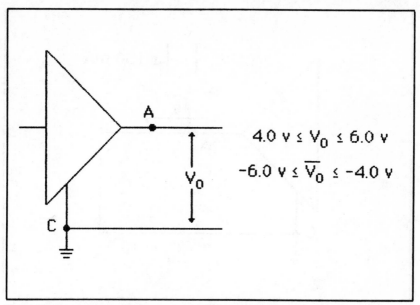

$$4.0 \text{ v} \leq V_0 \leq 6.0 \text{ v}$$

$$-6.0 \text{ v} \leq \overline{V_0} \leq -4.0 \text{ v}$$

Fig. 8-13. Open-circuit voltage specifications for RS-423-A unbalanced drivers.

to the receiver inputs, the resulting currents must lie within the shaded region shown in Fig. 8-12.

The electrical parameters of the RS-423-A unbalanced drivers are illustrated in Figs. 8-13 through 8-16. Tables 8-4 and 8-5 list IC driver circuits suitable for RS-422-A and RS-423-A respectively. Table 8-6 lists a number of IC receiver circuits that can be used for either RS-422-A or RS-423-A.

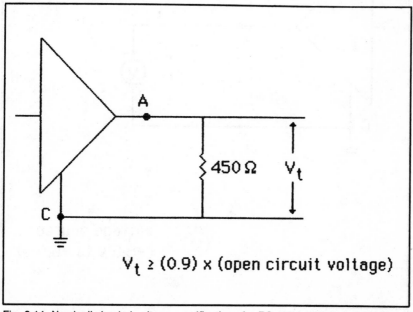

$$V_t \geq (0.9) \times (\text{open circuit voltage})$$

Fig. 8-14. Nominally-loaded voltage specifications for RS-423-A unbalanced drives.

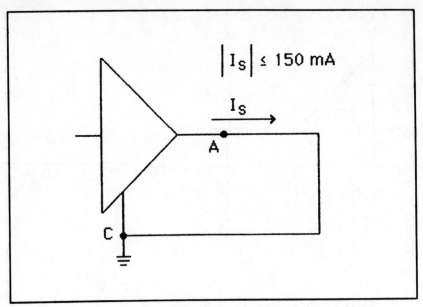

Fig. 8-15. Short-circuit current specification for RS-423-A unbalanced drivers.

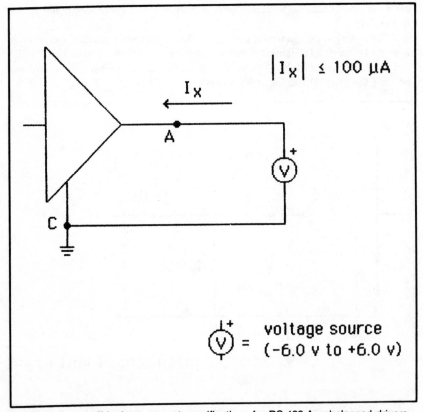

Fig. 8-16. Power-off leakage current specifications for RS-423-A unbalanced drivers.

Table 8-4. IC Drivers for RS-422-A.

AMD	AM26LS30C
	AM26LS31C
Fairchild	9634C
Motorola	MC3487
	AM26LS31
National	DS8832
	DS3487
	DS26LS31C
	DS1691
Signetics	AM26LS30
	AM26LS31
Texas Instruments	SN75151
	SN75158
	SN75159
	SN75172
	SN75174
	MC3487
	AM26LS31C
	μA9639C

ELECTRICAL INTEROPERATION WITH RS-232-C

As we said before, RS-449, RS-422-A, and RS-423-A are improved standards which together are intended to replace RS-232-C. However, there is a very large and still growing installed base of RS-232-C equipment that is not likely to disappear for many many years. To promote changeover to the new standards in new equipment designs, they were developed to permit the design of compliant equipment that is still capable of a large degree of interoperation with existing RS-232-C equipment. The EIA recommendations and guidelines regarding this interoperability are contained in *Industrial Electronics Bulletin No. 12—Application Notes On Interconnection Between Interface Circuits Using RS-449 and RS-232-C (IEB-12)*.

Table 8-5. IC Drivers for RS-423-A.

AMD	AM26LS29C
	AM26LS30C
Fairchild	9636AC
Motorola	MC3487
National	DS3487
	DS1691
Signetics	AM26LS29
	AM26LS30
Texas Instruments	MC3487
	µA9639C
	µA9636A

Table 8-6. IC Receivers for RS-422-A and RS-423-A.

AMD	AM26LS32C
Fairchild	9637AC
Motorola	MC3486
National	DS26LS32C
	DS3486
Texas Instruments	SN75157
	µA9637AC
	MC3486
	AM26LS32C
	SN75173
	SN75175

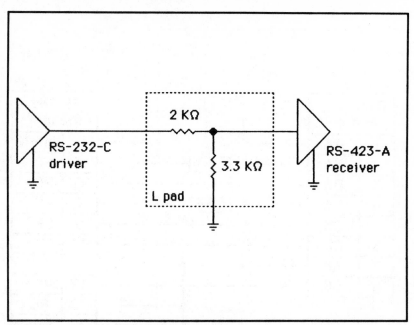

Fig. 8-17. L pad attenuator for interfacing an RS-232-C driver to an RS-423-A receiver.

Since RS-423-A receivers need only withstand ±12 volts on their inputs and RS-232-C drivers can supply up to ±25 volts, an *L pad attenuator* shown in Fig. 8-17 should be inserted in each interface circuit that is driven by the RS-232-C equipment. To minimize crosstalk from adjacent circuits, this pad should be located within ten cable feet of the RS-449 equipment. Waveshaping is another area that requires some attention. RS-232-C only implicitly addresses the issue of rise and fall times by specifying that a transitioning signal only spend the lesser of one millisecond or 4% of a bit time within the transition region between −3 volts and +3 volts. RS-423-A specifies that the rise and fall times between 10% and 90% of full voltage be less than the smaller of 300 microseconds or 30% of a bit time. These two different requirements are analytically compared in IEB-12, but for practical purposes the "bottom line" is that interoperation is possible at rates up to 19.2 kbps with linear waveshaping and a risetime of 2.2 microseconds.

Although IEB-12 states that direct interoperation between RS-422-A and RS-232-C is not possible, this may not always be the case. As we will see upon examining the Macintosh serial I/O structure in Chapter 15, certain driver and receiver circuits are capable of supporting communications with either RS-422-A or RS-232-C equipment.

FUNCTIONAL INTEROPERATION WITH RS-232-C

In addition to the electrical and timing requirements, certain differences in interface circuit functionality must be dealt with, since there is not an exact one-to-one correspondence between RS-449 and RS-232-C logical interface circuits. Figures 8-18 and 8-19 show the recommended adaptor configurations for connecting the primary and secondary circuits of an RS-232-C terminal to an RS-449 modem. Adaptor configurations for connecting RS-449 terminals to RS-232-C modems are shown in Figs. 8-20 and 8-21.

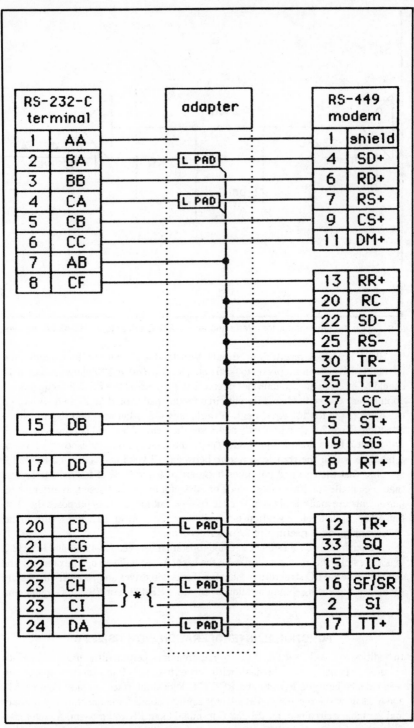

Fig. 8-18. Adapter configuration for connecting primary circuits of an RS-232-C terminal to an RS-449 modem.

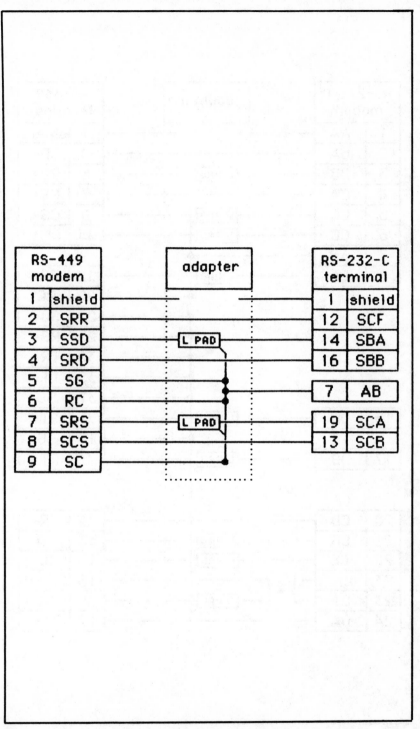

Fig. 8-19. Adapter configuration for connecting secondary circuits of an RS-232-C terminal to an RS-449 modem.

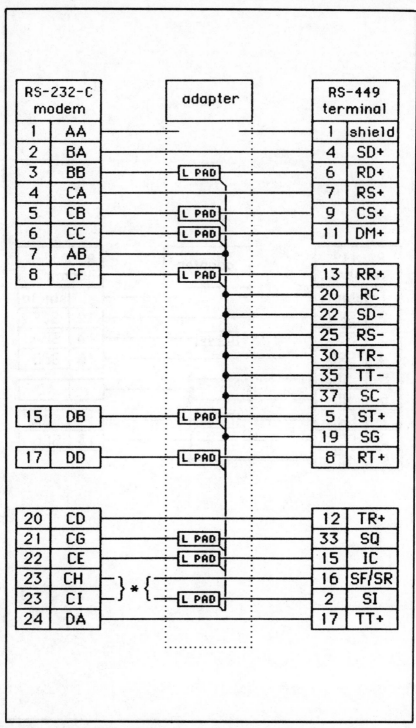

Fig. 8-20. Adapter configuration for connecting primary circuits of an RS-449 terminal to an RS-232-C modem.

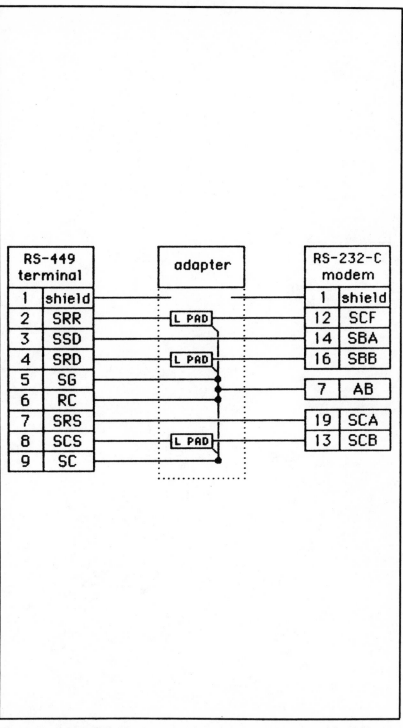

Fig. 8-21. Adapter configuration for connecting secondary circuits of an RS-449 terminal to an RS-232-C modem.

Chapter 9

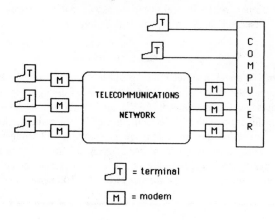

$\boxed{\lrcorner T}$ = terminal

$\boxed{M}$ = modem

Modems

T HE THEORETICAL ASPECTS OF MODULATION TECHNIQUES USED IN DATA TRANS-
mission were discussed in Chapter 6. The present chapter concerns *modems*,
which are the practical devices used to modulate and demodulate digital data for
transmission over various media. (Most Bell System literature refers to modems as
data sets.) Specifically we will examine the widely used Bell System 103, 113, 201,
202, 212, 208, and 209 standards along with CCITT recommendations V.21 and V.23.
But first, we will look at some features common to many different models.

FULL-DUPLEX, HALF-DUPLEX, AND SIMPLEX

A great confusion exists over the correct usage of *full-duplex, half-duplex,* and *simplex*
in describing modem capabilities. This confusion is perhaps fueled by the fact that
"correct" usage in North America is different from the "correct" usage defined by
the International Telecommunications Union (ITU), which is a United Nations agency
and the parent organization of CCITT. In North America, *simplex* refers to communications circuits that can transmit in only one direction. *Half-duplex* circuits are capable
of transmitting in either direction, but only in a single direction at one time. *Full-
duplex* circuits can transmit in both directions simultaneously. According to ITU usage, simplex circuits are capable of transmitting in either direction but only in a single
direction at one time. Half-duplex circuits are inherently capable of full-duplex operation but are restricted to transmitting in one direction at a time due to the limitations of the terminal equipment. ANSI completely avoids the confusing terminology
by categorizing circuit operation as either *one-way only, two-way alternate,* or *two-way
simultaneous.* This book will stick to either the North American or ANSI terminology.

ECHO SUPPRESSOR DISABLING

As discussed in Chapter 5, most long haul telephone circuits are equipped with *echo suppressors* that must be disabled when the circuits are used for data transmission, and many modems are equipped with circuitry to provide the necessary disabling tone of the proper frequency and duration. Most echo suppressors will be disabled by a 400 millisecond single-frequency tone falling between 2010 and 2240 Hz.

BELL 103/113

Bell System 103 and 113 series modems operate asynchronously at up to 300 baud using frequency-shift keying. As shown in Fig. 9-1, full-duplex operation of the 103 series requires two different pairs of MARK and SPACE frequencies—one for transmission in each direction. The SPACE frequency of 1070 Hz and the MARK frequency of 1270 Hz are called the *originate* frequencies and a 103 modem transmitting on them is operating in the *originate mode*. The SPACE frequency of 2025 Hz and the MARK frequency of 2225 Hz are called the *answer* frequencies and a modem transmitting on them is operating in the *answer mode*. All 103 series modems are capable

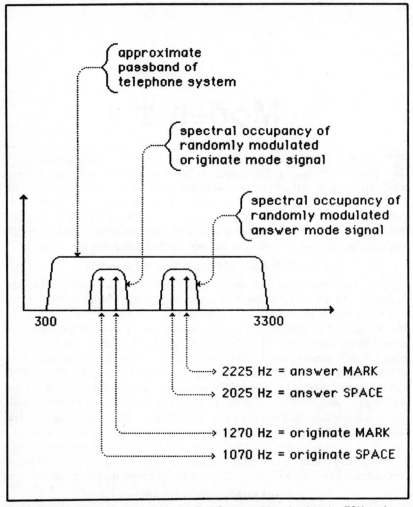

Fig. 9-1. Frequency assignments used in Bell System 103 and 113 series FSK modems.

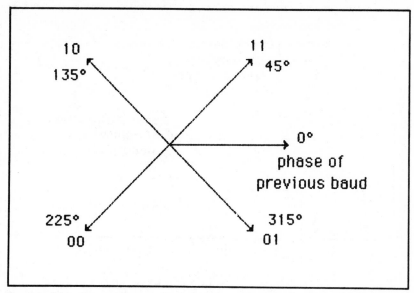

Fig. 9-2. Dibit phase shift assignments used in Bell System 201B and 201C DPSK modems.

of operation in either answer or originate mode. For remote terminal installations that always originate calls, the answer mode capability will be superfluous and it may be more economical to use the less complicated 113A or 113C modems that can only operate in the originate mode. Conversely, at a host computer site that only answers calls, it will be advantageous to use 113B or 113D answer-only modems. Series 103 units operating in answer mode can communicate with either 103 modems operating in originate mode or with 113A or 113C originate-only modems. Likewise 103 units operating in originate mode are compatible with either other 103 series units or 113B or 113D answer-only units. The 2225 Hz answer mode MARK tone of 113B, 113D, and 103 series units can be used for echo suppressor disabling.

BELL 201

Bell System 201B and 201C modems employ four-level differential phase-shift-keying (DPSK) to provide synchronous communications at 2400 bits per second by sending dibit symbols at 1200 baud. In DPSK, each dibit is encoded in the amount of phase shift from one transmitted symbol to the next as shown in Fig. 9-2. Model 201B is for leased line use and 201C is for dial-up lines.

BELL 202

Bell System 202 series modems employ frequency-shift keying operating at 1200 bps on dial-up lines, at 1400 bps on leased lines with C1 conditioning, and at 1800 bps on leased lines with C2 conditioning. As shown in Fig. 9-3, 2200 Hz is transmitted for SPACE and 1200 is transmitted for MARK. A reverse signaling channel is provided in models 202C6, 202C10, and 202C12 by on-off keying of a 397 Hz carrier at a rate of five baud. As discussed in Chapter 6, the bandwidth of a voice-grade telephone line will only accommodate one pair of frequencies capable of 1200 baud FSK transmission. Therefore, only half-duplex operation is possible on two-wire cir-

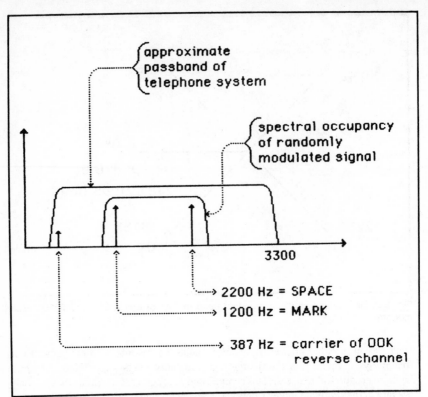

Fig. 9-3. Frequency assignments used in Bell System 202 series FSK modems.

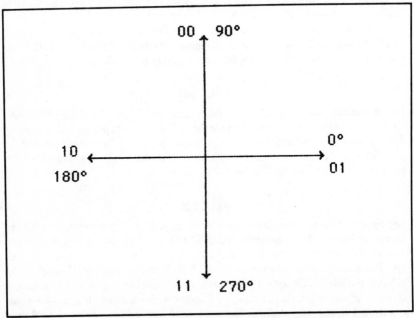

Fig. 9-4. Dibit phase shift assignments used in Bell System 212A PSK modem.

cuits such as the switched telephone network. However full-duplex operation on four-wired leased circuits is possible with models 202D, 202R, and 202T.

BELL 212A

The Bell 212A modem can communicate asynchronously at 300 bps using 103 series compatible FSK and at 1200 bps using four-level PSK to send 600 dibits per second. The frequency assignments for 300 bps operation are identical to those for 103 series modems shown in Fig. 9-1. The phase assigned to each dibit for 1200 bps operation is shown in Fig. 9-4. The answer mode carrier frequency is 2400 Hz, and the originate carrier frequency is 1200 Hz. The 212A standard is the predominant 1200 bps modem in the small computer communications arena.

BELL 208

Bell System 208 series modems employ eight-level phase-shift keying (PSK) to provide synchronous communication at 4800 bits per second by sending tribit symbols at 1600 baud. The phase shift assigned to each tribit is shown in Fig. 9-5. The 208A modem operates in either half-duplex or full-duplex over a four-wire leased line. The 209B operates in half-duplex over the dial-up network.

BELL 209A

The 209A modem provides 9600 bps communications using a combination of PSK and ASK called *quadrature amplitude modulation* (QAM) to transmit 2400 quadbit symbols per second over DI-conditioned four-wire leased lines. The amplitude and phase assigned to each quadbit is shown in Fig. 9-6.

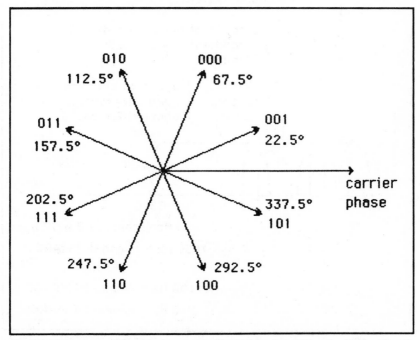

Fig. 9-5. Tribit phase shift assignments used in Bell System 208 series PSK modems.

113

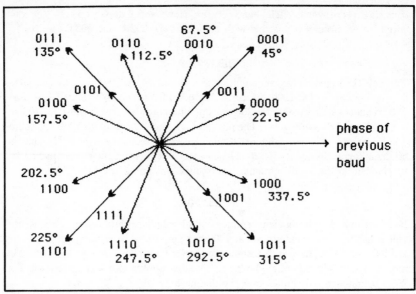

Fig. 9-6. Quadbit amplitude and phase shift assignments used in Bell System 209A modem.

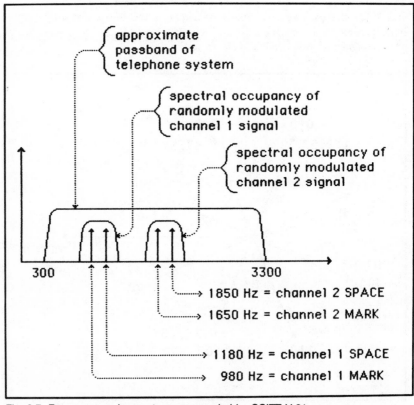

Fig. 9-7. Frequency assignments recommended by CCITT V.21.

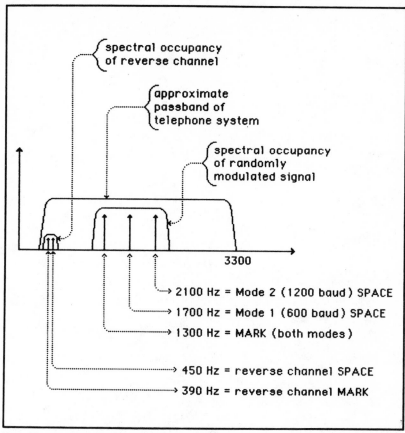

spectral occupancy
of reverse channel

approximate
passband of
telephone system

spectral occupancy
of randomly
modulated signal

3300

⟶ 2100 Hz = Mode 2 (1200 baud) SPACE

⟶ 1700 Hz = Mode 1 (600 baud) SPACE

⟶ 1300 Hz = MARK (both modes)

⟶ 450 Hz = reverse channel SPACE

⟶ 390 Hz = reverse channel MARK

Fig. 9-8. Frequency assignments recommended by CCITT V.23.

CCITT V.21

CCITT Recommendation V.21 concerns 200 bps modems for full-duplex operation in the switched telephone network. The transmission method employed is an FSK scheme similar to Bell 103. The frequency assignments are shown in Fig. 9-7.

CCITT V.23

CCITT Recommendation V.23 concerns 600 to 1200 bps modems for half-duplex operation in the switched telephone network. As shown in Fig. 9-8, the MARK frequency is 1300 Hz and the SPACE frequency is either 1700 Hz or 2100 Hz depending on whether the maximum data rate is 600 or 1200 baud. An optional reverse channel provides 75 bps communications in the reverse direction using 390 Hz for MARK and 450 Hz for SPACE.

Chapter 10

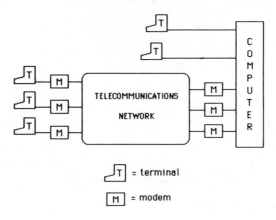

$\boxed{\text{T}}$ = terminal

$\boxed{\text{M}}$ = modem

Multiplexers

IN MANY APPLICATIONS THERE WILL BE A NEED FOR SEVERAL RELATIVELY LOW-speed channels running between two installations. Due to the pricing structure of common carrier facilities used for the long haul links between the sites, however, the total cost of a few low-capacity links will usually be much higher than a single link having a capacity equal to or greater than the sum of all the slower links. As depicted in Fig. 10-1, the economics of this fact can be exploited with the aid of a *multiplexer,* which is a device for combing a number of data signals into a single higher-bandwidth signal. Two basic techniques for multiplexing wireline data signals are *time division multiplexing* (TDM) and *frequency division multiplexing* (FDM).

TIME DIVISION MULTIPLEXING

The basic idea behind time division multiplexing is shown in Fig. 10-2. The individual bits in a number of user channels are spread apart and interleaved to form a single composite bit stream for long-haul transmission. When it comes to practical working systems, there are several variations on this basic idea. In *synchronous TDM*, the data clocks of the individual user signals are all derived from a master clock that is provided by either the multiplexer or a modem connected to the composite side of the multiplexer as shown in Fig. 10-3. On the other hand, in *asynchronous TDM* the data transfers from the individual users to the multiplexer make use of an asynchronous start-stop format as discussed in Chapter 4. While this permits increased flexibility in selection of individual terminal devices, it complicates the multiplexer design since a number of different user data streams of different and arbitrarily related data rates must be combined into a single, constant rate composite data stream.

Isochronous TDM can be viewed as sort of a compromise between synchronous

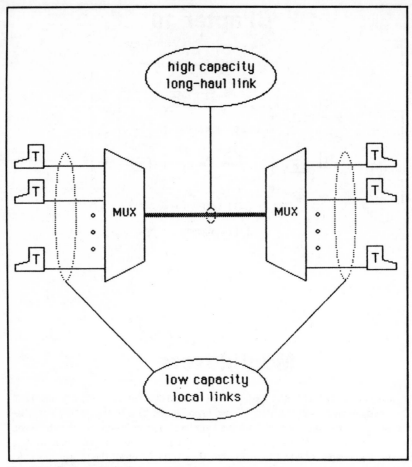

Fig. 10-1. Basic multiplexing.

and asynchronous approaches. The individual terminals each generate their own clocks, but all of these clocks are running at the same nominal rate. Unlike synchronous multiplexers, isochronous multiplexers must provide some buffering and rate smoothing to compensate for slight differences between the various user clock rates. However, the differences are relatively small and can be accommodated much more easily than the extreme variations possible in asynchronous approaches.

MULTIPOINT MULTIPLEXING

Assume that we wish to connect several terminals located in New York and Denver to a host mainframe located in San Francisco, as depicted in Fig. 10-4. One of the terminals in New York will be used exclusively for communicating with one of the terminals in Denver. Let's assume there are a total of three 300 baud terminals in New York and three 150 baud terminals plus one 300 baud terminal in Denver. Furthermore, assume that we can only afford one 1200 baud link from New York to Denver and one 1200 baud link from Denver to San Francisco. Terminal A in New York needs to talk to terminal G in Denver, while all of the remaining terminals talk to the mainframe in San Francisco. This can be accomplished as shown in Fig. 10-5 by using

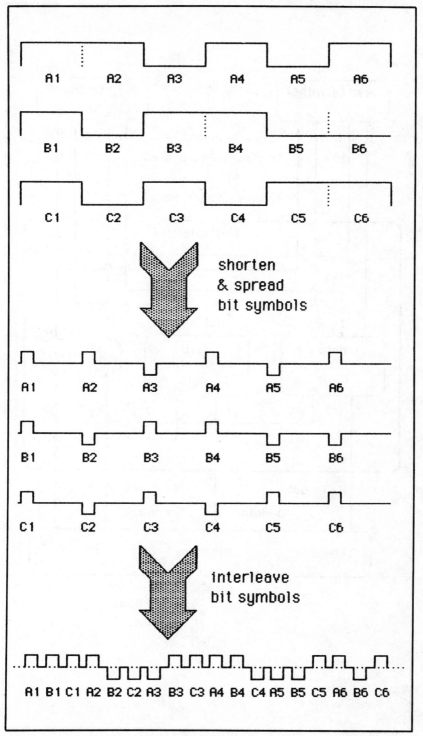

Fig. 10-2. Fundamentals of time division multiplexing.

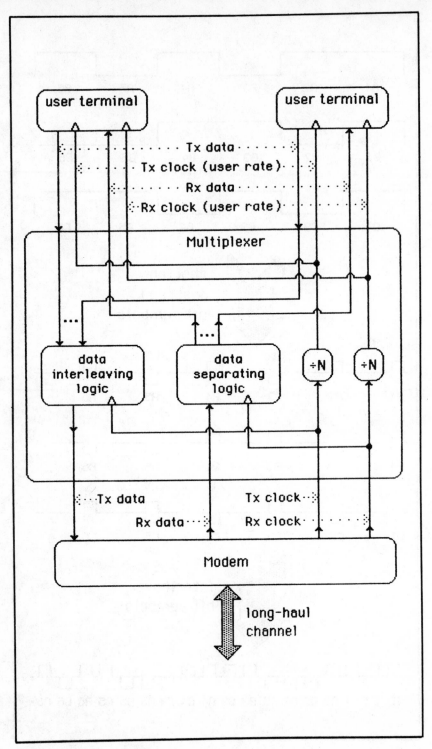

Fig. 10-3. Synchronous TDM.

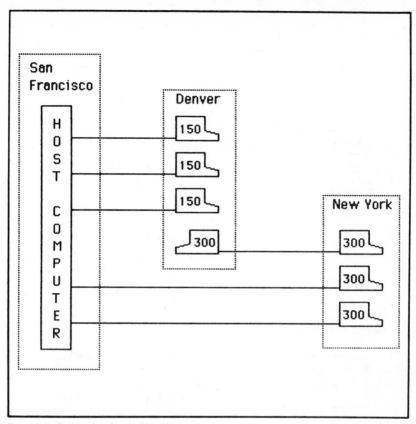

Fig. 10-4. A situation for multipoint multiplexing.

either four "regular" TD multiplexers or as shown in Fig. 10-6 by using one multitrunk TD multiplexer (at Denver) plus two "regulars. Either approach requires the duplication of a lot of common circuitry just so that the Denver equipment can synchronize with the New York and San Francisco data streams in order to locate inbound data to be extracted and to locate windows in which to insert outbound data. Applications such as this, involving multiuser communications between two locations (new York and San Francisco) with some users added and some dropped at an intermediate location (Denver), are often more economically served using an FDM rather than TDM approach.

FREQUENCY DIVISION MULTIPLEXING

In frequency division multiplexing, a number of relatively narrowband, low-capacity signals are modulated onto a number of carriers at different frequencies located within the passband of a relatively wideband *composite channel* as shown in Fig. 10-7. After the composite signal is transmitted to the destination site, the individual user channels must be demultiplexed and put in a baseband form suitable for interfacing to the appropriate terminal equipment. Our multipoint example of Fig. 10-4 is fairly simple to implement with FDM. The demultiplexing equipment in Denver can simply demodulate that part of the composite spectrum that contains the data inbound for Denver without disturbing (or having to synchronize with) data that is just "passing through" to one of the other cities. Likewise, the multiplexing equipment can

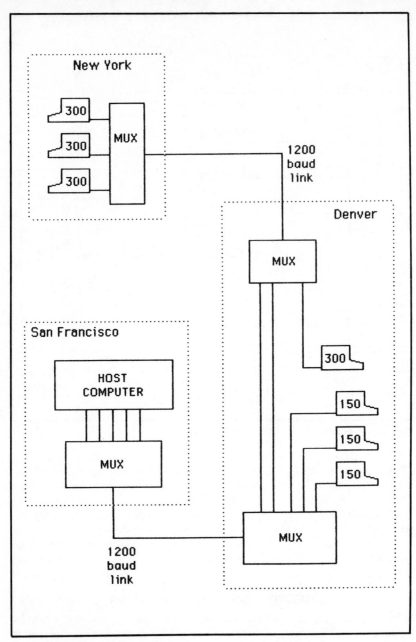

Fig. 10-5. Multipoint TD multiplexing.

simply modulate outbound data into the appropriate channel within the composite spectrum without regard for the contents of the other channels. FDM systems are widespread throughout the telephone industry and in multipoint multiplexing applications, but for point-to-point multiplexing of data traffic, TDM techniques are often more attractive due to the simpler and more reliable all-digital multiplexer designs that are possible.

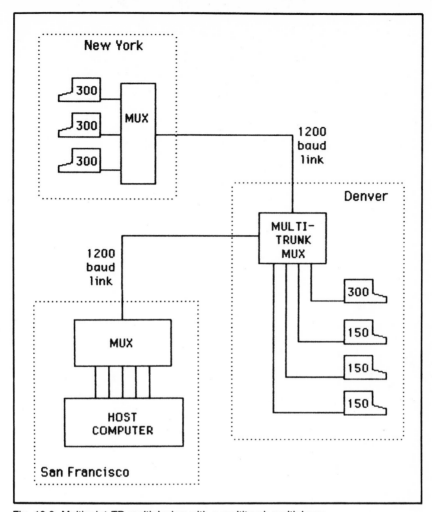

Fig. 10-6. Multipoint TD multiplexing with a multitrunk multiplexer.

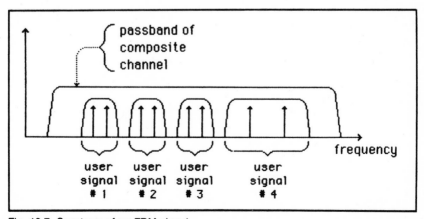

Fig. 10-7. Spectrum of an FDM signal.

Chapter 11

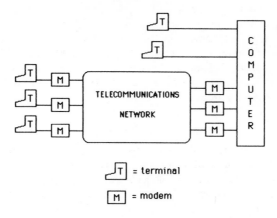

T = terminal

M = modem

Character-Oriented
Data-Link Protocols

A S DISCUSSED IN CHAPTER 1, PROTOCOLS FOR DATA-LINK CONTROL ARE CON-cerned with the logical aspects of transmitting data over the physical links selected and established by network layer and physical layer protocols. Until fairly recently, most practical data-link control (DLC) protocols have been *character-oriented*, using defined sequences of special characters to frame the data characters and control their exchange between the communicating stations. Most hobbyist and other longstanding data-link protocols were developed on a more or less ad hoc basis using character-oriented techniques, since formal standards did not exist. As is the case with many IBM practices, the IBM *Binary Synchronous Communications* (Bisync) protocol filled the void and became a de facto standard. In 1971 formal standardization finally arrived with the publication of ANSI standard X3.28. A significantly updated version was released in 1976 and is still in use today.

In this chapter, we will first discuss some structure and functional requirements common to all character-oriented protocols before examining the procedural elements of ANSI X3.28; IBM Bisync; and XMODEM, which is a highly popular hobbyist protocol.

FUNDAMENTAL REQUIREMENTS

As discussed in previous chapters, extremely long messages are likely to become corrupted by errors when transmitted through real-world communications facilities. However shorter messages can and do survive such transmissions with fairly high regularity. Therefore one of the major functions of DLC protocols is to provide a means for breaking up long messages into shorter blocks which are more suitable for successful transmission through typical facilities. Of course, some blocks will still experience errors and the DLC protocols must include measures for detecting and correcting these errors.

In all but the most trivial two-station, point-to-point configuration the DLC protocol must also provide a means for identifying the particular stations involved in an exchange of data. Furthermore, the DLC protocol must provide a way to acquire and maintain character or byte synchronization between the sender and receiver. The various techniques of character synchronization were discussed in Chapter 4, but selection and implementation of a particular one is a matter to be addressed in data-link control specifications.

DATA TRANSPARENCY

A major consideration in the design of DLC protocols is *data transparency*, the ability to successfully transmit data with bit patterns which may coincidentally match the bit patterns of communications control characters used to delimit data and control link operation. For instance we may wish to include the single byte integer value of $(4)_{dec} = (00000100)_{bin}$. Unfortunately this is exactly the same bit pattern exhibited by a no-parity ASCII EOT character, and unless special precautions are taken the receiving station will interpret it as such and act accordingly. In most character-oriented DLCs, data transparency is achieved by using a data link escape (DLE) in conjunction with the other communications control characters. Operating under transparent-data protocols a receiving station will interpret each received byte as pure data unless it is preceded by a DLE character. If a data byte resembling DLE (00010000) is to be sent, it will be sent as two consecutive DLE characters.

WATCHDOG TIMERS

Many DLC protocols are based on one station transmitting a block of date and then waiting for a response from the receiving station before deciding upon the next action to be taken. For example, if the response indicates that the received block contained errors the sending station will usually retransmit the same block over again. On the other hand, if the response indicates that the block was received without errors, the sender can proceed on to transmit the next block in the message. This technique can be very useful, but it suffers from a serious drawback—if the response message becomes garbled or lost in transmission, the original sending station can wind up waiting forever. To guard against this, a sending station that expects a reply must run a *response timer* that will expire or *time out* if a reply is not received within a reasonable period. A similar problem can occur if an end-of-black or end-of message delimiting character (ETX, ETB, TETX, etc.) becomes garbled. In this case the receiving station will never recognize that a response is called for and hence will never provide one. Although this condition would eventually result in expiration of the response timer at the original sending station, more efficient recovery procedures can be realized if the receiving station starts a *receive timer* which will expire if the ending delimiter is not recognized within a reasonable period of time. Timers, such as response timers and receive timers, used to safeguard link operation are sometimes called *watchdog timers*.

XMODEM

In early 1878, Ward Christensen and Randy Suess started the Chicago computerized Bulletin Board System (CBBS). One of the features of this CBBS was a program called MODEM which allowed file exchanges between CP/M computers. Improvements were made to MODEM and various descendants are known as XMODEM, MODEM7,

MODEM7A, and TMODEM. These programs plus a number of commercially developed programs support a common file transfer protocol which has become a de facto standard on RCPM systems. There is nothing inherent in the XMODEM communications protocol which would preclude its use in non-CP/M systems, however some operating systems might need to do the local file handling, disk operations, and features somewhat differently.

XMODEM divides the file to be sent into blocks which each contain 128 bytes of data. As shown in Fig. 11-1, a start-of-header (ASCII SOH), two block-number bytes, and a checksum byte are added to the data bytes to form a complete block for transmission. In some implementations, two CRC bytes are used in lieu of the single checksum byte. (See Chapter 2 for a discussion of checksums and cyclic-redundancy checking.) Upon receiving a block, the receiving station will compute the checksum/CRC and compare it with the one contained in the transmitted block. If the two values agree, the receiving station will send an affirmative acknowledgment (ASCII ACK) to the sending station. Upon receipt of the ACK, the sending station will proceed to send the next block of data. On the other hand, if the checksum/CRC is incorrect, the receiving station will send a negative acknowledgment (ASCII NAK) to the sending station. Upon receipt of the NAK, the sending station will transmit the same block over again. the checksum or CRC will safeguard the integrity of the entire block but both are unable to pinpoint the location within the block of a detected error. Transmission errors could occur in the SOH character, in the block number, in the data, or in the checksum byte itself. Normally, the inability to discriminate between these error conditions would not be significant since the usual recovery procedure involves a NAK response followed by a retransmission of the erroneous block. However suppose that the sending station transmits a block which is successfully received. The receiving station will store the data away and transmit ACK to the sender. If this ACK becomes garbled or lost, a watchdog timer in the sender will expire causing the sender to assume that the original transmission never got through. The sender will then retransmit the block in question. If this block then becomes garbled in transmission the checksum/CRC test will fail at the receiver and the receiver should respond with NAK. This will be somewhat inefficient, however, since the receiver has already successfully received the original transmission of this same block. Instead of responding with NAK, the receiver could send ACK, thus permitting the sender to proceed to the next block. There is one small problem with this idea though—suppose checksum/CRC failure is due to an error in the block number? This is the reason two block-number bytes are used—the first one is just the block number (0 to 255), while the second byte is the one's complement of the first. If these two bytes are exclusive-ORed together the result must always be equal to $(FF)_{hex}$. Thus, a single error occurring in either one of the block-number bytes will cause the XOR result to be something different, allowing the receiver to distinguish between block number errors and errors in the data or checksum bytes.

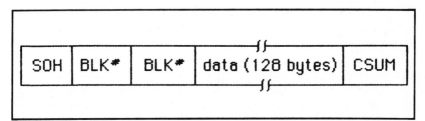

Fig. 11-1. XMODEM message format.

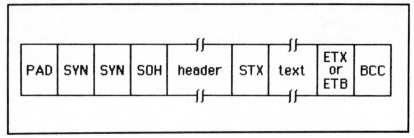

Fig. 11-2. Bisync message format.

IBM BISYNC

In the early 1960's, IBM developed a synchronous DLC protocol called *Binary Synchronous Communications* (BSC or Bisync). This protocol was designed to work with either EBCDIC or ASCII codes instead of the *four-out-of-eight* code used in earlier synchronous DLC efforts by IBM. Bisync achieves operation with either EBCDIC or ASCII by restricting communications control characters to those that are common to both codes. The Bisync message format is shown in Fig. 11-2. PAD is a special character consisting of alternate ones and zeros used to help the receiving station accomplish bit synchronization prior to the arrival of the actual message. As discussed in Chapter 4, the SYN characters are used to establish character or byte synchronization. Data transparency is achieved by use of data-link escape (DLE) techniques discussed earlier in this chapter. In newer implementations, the block check character (BCC) is sometimes replaced by two CRC bytes.

ANSI X3.28

ANSI Standard X3.28, "American National Standard Procedures for the Use of the Communication Control Characters of American National Standard Code for Information Interchange in Specified Data Communications Links" is not a single protocol but rather a collection of control procedures for a variety of applications and system configurations. These procedures are divided into what ANSI calls "subcategories." Some of these subcategories specify protocols for establishment and termination of communications on various link configurations, while others specify protocols for various types of message transfer. The message transfer subcategories are listed in Table 11-1 and the establishment and termination subcategories are listed in Table 11-2. Notice that the message transfer subcategory designations begin with a letter, while designations for establishment and termination subcategories begin with a number. We will take a closer look at subcategories 2.2 and B2 since these are fairly representative of the techniques and methodologies throughout X3.28.

CONTROL SEQUENCE EXTENSIONS

In order to extend the control capabilities of the ASCII communications control characters (see Table 2-10), ANSI X3.28 uses the data-link escape character, DLE, to form a number of control sequence code extensions which are listed in Table 11-3 and discussed in the paragraphs below.

Mandatory Disconnect (DEOT = "DLE EOT") is sent by a master station to indicate the end of a transmission and initiate a disconnect of a circuit-switched communications channel.

Acknowledgment N (ACKN = "DLE n", n = 0, 1, 2, 3, 4, 5, 6, or 7) is used in

Table 11-1. Message Transfer Subcategories of ANSI X3.28.

	message-oriented	message-associated blocking	message-independent blocking	conversational	replies	one-/character acknowledgments	alternating acknowledgments	modulo-8 acknowledgments	longitudinal checking	CRC checking	full duplex	data transparency	batch transmission
A1	*												
A2	*								*				
A3	*				*								
A4	*				*				*				
B1		*				*			*				
B2		*					*		*				
C1			*			*			*				
C2			*					*	*				
D1			*				*			*		*	
E1				*									
E2				*					*				
E3				*					*				*
F1		*					*		*		*		
F2			*					*	*		*		

lieu of ACK for an affirmative reply when an acknowledgment numbering capability is required. In some subcategories a prefix containing supplementary information may precede ACKN.

Start of Transmission Block (SOTB = "DLE =") is used to indicate the start of a block of data for communications purposes when the block structure need not be related to the ultimate processing format. In some subcategories it is implicit that a block number immediately follows SOTB.

Transparent Start of Heading (TSOH = "DLE SOH") is used to indicate the start of a transparent heading or the start of a continuation block of a transparent heading. (A transparent heading is one that may contain bytes of data that look like ASCII communications control characters, but are to be interpreted only as data.) The heading will typically contain address and routing information for the message.

129

Table 11-2. Establishment and Termination Subcategories of ANSI X3.28.

	simplex	half duplex	full duplex	point-to-point	multipoint	switched	nonswitched	centralized control	noncentralized control	station ID procedures	single slave	multiple slaves	permanent master	polling/selection	contention
1.1	*			*		*					*		*		
2.1		*		*		*					*			*	
2.2		*		*		*				*	*			*	
2.3		*		*			*				*				*
2.4		*			*			*			*			*	
2.5		*			*			*			*			*	
2.6		*			*				*		*			*	
2.7		*			*			*				*		*	
2.8		*			*				*			*		*	
3.1			*	*						*					

Transparent Start of Text (TSTX = "DLE STX") is used to indicate the start of a block of transparent text. If a transparent heading is used, it is terminated with TSTX.

Transparent End of Text (TETX = "DLE ETX") is used to terminate the final block of transparent text contained in a message. In some subcategories it is implicit that two CRC bytes immediately follow TETX.

Transparent End of Block (TETB = "DLE ETB") is used to terminate transparent blocks of heading or text which are not final blocks in the message. In some subcategories it is implicit that two CRC bytes immediately follow TETB.

Transparent Synchronous Idle (TSYN = "DLE SYN") is used in lieu of SYN when transparent data is being sent.

Transparent DLE (TDLE = "DLE DLE") is used to send the DLE bit pattern in transparent data.

Wait After Positive Acknowledgment (WACK = "DLE ;") is used in lieu of ACK when that would be the appropriate response except for the unreadiness of the receiver to receive the next block of data. In some subcategories an optional prefix may precede WACK, and in some WACK may be used in lieu of ACKO.

Start of Supervisory Sequence (SOSS = "DLE :") is used in two-way simulataneous protocols to indicate the beginning of a slave's protocol-required response which is embedded in a transmission of regular data.

Transparent Block Abort (TENQ = "DLE ENQ") is used to abort transparent data being transmitted.

Reverse Interrupt (RINT = "DLE <") is used in lieu of ACK when the responding station wishes to make a positive acknowledgment and request a reversal of the link direction.

POINT-TO-POINT, HALF-DUPLEX COMMUNICATIONS VIA SWITCHED CIRCUITS

Subcategory 2.1 of ANSI X3.28 consists of procedures for establishment and termination of two-way alternate (half duplex) communications via point-to-point connections in a circuit-switched network. This is precisely the situation that exists in many remote terminal applications that depend on the dialup telephone network for connection to a distant host computer service. The standard does not deal directly with auto dialing or signaling protocols needed to establish the physical telephone circuit connection. However, once the connection is established by autodialing equipment or human intervention, the calling station assumes the role of master station and is free to begin executing the protocol that contains the following elements (The step numbers correspond to the branch in Fig. 11-3.)

Table 11-3. ANSI X3.28 Control Sequence Code Extensions.

Extension Symbol	Character Sequence	Definition
DEOT	DLE EOT	Mandatory Disconnect
ACKO	DLE 0	Acknowledgment 0
ACK1	DLE 1	Acknowledgment 1
ACK2	DLE 2	Acknowledgment 2
ACK3	DLE 3	Acknowledgment 3
ACK4	DLE 4	Acknowledgment 4
ACK5	DLE 5	Acknowledgment 5
ACK6	DLE 6	Acknowledgment 6
ACK7	DLE 7	Acknowledgment 7
SOTB	DLE =	Start of Transmission Block
TSOH	DLE SOH	Transparent Start of Heading
TSTX	DLE STX	Transparent Start of Text
TETX	DLE ETX	Transparent End of Text
TETB	DLE ETB	Transparent End of Block
TSYN	DLE SYN	Transparent Synchronous Idle
TDLE	DLE DLE	Transparent DLE
WACK	DLE ;	Wait After Positive Ackn.
SOSS	DLE :	Start of Supervisory Sequence
TENQ	DLE ENQ	Transparent Block Abort
RINT	DLE <	Reverse Interrupt

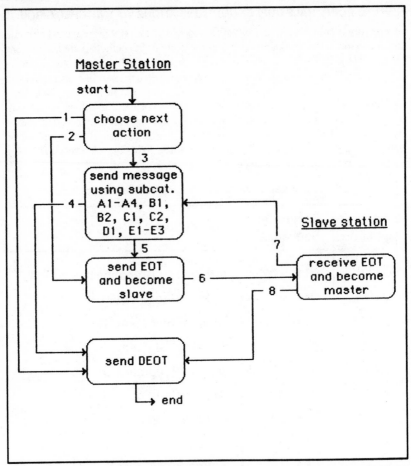

Fig. 11-3. Subcategory 2.1 establishment and termination procedures of ANSI X3.28.

1. Master has no message to send and proceeds to initiate a disconnect.

2. Master station may relinquish master status to slave station.

3. Master transmits message text using message transfer subcategory A1, A2, A3, A4, B1, B2, C1, C2, D1, E1, E2, or E3.

4. Not desiring a response, master proceeds to initiate a disconnect after message has been transferred.

5. Master sends EOT and assumes slave status.

6. Slave receives EOT and assumes master status.

7. After assuming master status, original slave having a message to send does so using message transfer subcategory A1, A2, A3, A4, B1, B2, C1, C2, D1, E1, E2, or E3.

8. After assuming master status, original slave having no response proceeds to initiate a disconnect.

SUBCATEGORY 2.2

Subcategory 2.2 is similar to subcategory 2.1 but it contains additional provisions for identification of the called station. (Refer to Fig. 11-4):

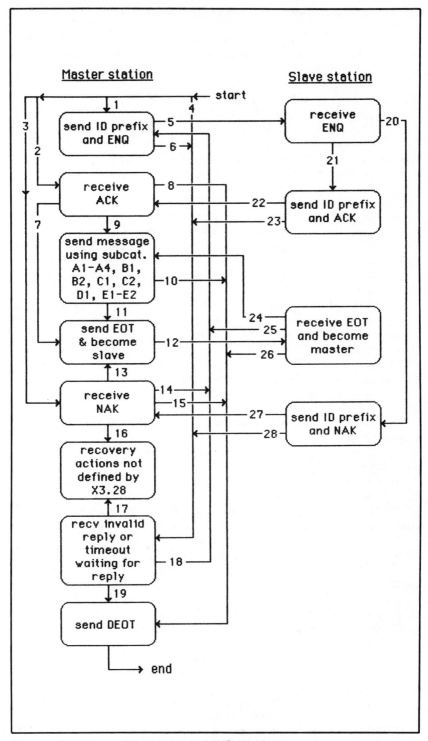

Fig. 11-4. Subcategory 2.2 procedures of ANSI X3.28.

1. After circuit is established, master sends an identification prefix followed by ENQ.

2. After circuit is established, master receives ACK from slave which is ready to receive. (This will occur in systems where initial ENQ is implied and slaves respond immediately upon circuit establishment.)

3. After circuit is established, master receives NAK from slave which is not ready to receive. (This will occur in systems where initial ENQ is implied and slaves respond immediately upon circuit establishment.)

4. After circuit is established, master receives an invalid response or times out waiting for response from slave. (This will occur in systems where initial ENQ is implied and slave respond immediately upon circuit establishment.)

5. Master's request for identification successfully reaches slave.

6. After sending request for identification, master receives an invalid response or times out waiting for a response.

7. After receiving ACK from slave, the master may send EOT thereby assuming slave status and authorizing slave to assume master status.

8. After receiving ACK from slave, the master may initiate a disconnect by sending DEOT.

9. After receiving ACK from slave, master may send message using message transfer subcategory A1, A2, A3, A4, B1, B2, C1, C2, D1, E1, E2, or E3.

10. After sending message, master may initiate a disconnect by sending DEOT.

11. After sending message, master may send EOT thereby assuming slave status and authorizing slave to assume master status.

12. EOT from abdicating master successfully reaches slave.

13. After receiving NAK from slave, master may send EOT thereby assuming slave status and authorizing slave to assume master status.

14. After receiving NAK from slave, master may repeat sending of identification prefix followed by ENQ.

15. After receiving NAK from slave, master may send DEOT thereby initiating a circuit disconnect.

16. After receiving NAK from slave, master may elect to execute recovery procedures that are not defined by X3.28.

17. After receiving an invalid response or timing out while waiting for a response, master may elect to execute recovery procedures that are not defined by X3.28.

18. After receiving an invalid response or timing out while waiting for a response, master may repeat sending of identification prefix followed by ENQ.

19. After receiving an invalid response or timing out while waiting for a response, master may send DEOT thereby initiating a circuit disconnect.

20. If slave station receives ENQ but is not ready to receive, it responds by sending an identification prefix followed by NAK.

21. If slave station receives ENQ and is ready to receive, it responds by sending an identification prefix following by ACK.

22. Slave's ACK response successfully reaches master.

23. Slave's ACK response becomes garbled or lost.

24. After receiving EOT from master, slave assumes master status and proceeds to send a message. (This is an option; in some systems slave may first execute identification sequence (25) before sending message.)

25. After receiving EOT from master, slave assumes master status and proceeds to send identification prefix followed by ENQ.

26. After receiving EOT from master, a slave having no message will initiate a disconnect by sending DEOT.

27. Slave's NAK response successfully reaches master.
28. Slave's NAK response becomes garbled or lost.

MESSAGE TRANSFER SUBCATEGORY B2

Subcategory B2 is a moderately complex example of the message transfer protocols defined by the subcategories of X3.28. The following procedure steps refer to the branches in Fig. 11-5:

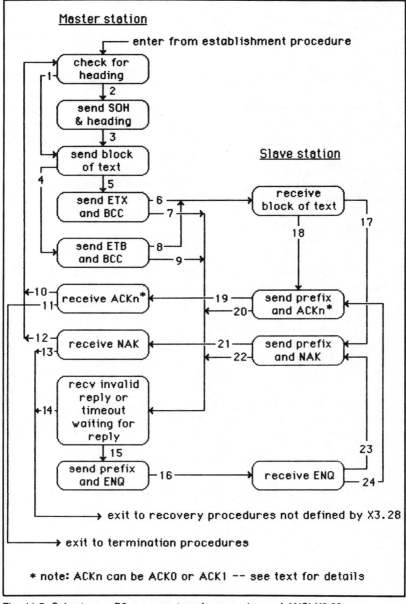

Fig. 11-5. Subcategory B2 message transfer procedures of ANSI X3.28.

1.If the message to be sent does not have a heading, the master sends STX followed by a block of text.

2. If the message to best has a heading, the master sends SOH followed by the heading.

3. After sending the heading, the master proceeds to send STX followed by a block of text.

4. A block of text that does not end the message is terminated by ETB followed by a block-check character.

5. A block of text that ends a message is terminated by ETX followed by a block-check character.

6. Block of text successfully reaches slave.

7. Master receives an invalid response or times out waiting for a response from slave.

8. Block of text successfully reaches slave.

9. Master receives an invalid response or times out waiting for a response from slave.

10. After receiving affirmative acknowledgment (ACK0 or ACK1) from the slave, the master will proceed to transmit a block of text. If the particular ACKN received is the correct one, the master will transmit the next block of text. If the particular ACKN received is incorrect, the master will treat it as a negative acknowledgment and transmit the same block over again.

11. If a correct ACKN is not received after a number of tries, the master may proceed to execute a recovery procedure that is not defined by X3.28.

12. After receiving negative acknowledgment (NAK) from the slave, the master will proceed to retransmit the same block.

13. If the master continues to receive NAK after a number of retries, the master may proceed to execute a recovery procedure that is not defined by X3.28.

14. After receiving an invalid response or timing out while waiting for a response, master may elect to execute recovery procedures that are not defined by X3.28.

15. After receiving an invalid response or timing out while waiting for a response, master may elect to send a reply request prefix followed by ENQ.

16. Reply-request prefix and ENQ successfully reach slave.

17. If the block-check character indicates that there is an error in the received block, the slave will send a response prefix followed by NAK.

18. If a block is received without errors, the slave will send a response prefix followed by ACK.

19. Slaves's ACK response successfully reaches master.

20. Slaves's ACK response becomes garbled or lost, causing master's response timer to expire.

21. Slave's NAK response successfully reaches master.

22. Slave's NAK response becomes garbled or lost, causing master's response timer to expire.

23. Upon receiving ENQ, a slave whose last response was NAK proceeds to re-send the same NAK response.

24. Upon receiving ENQ, a slave whose last response was ACK proceeds to re-send the same ACK response.

Chapter 12

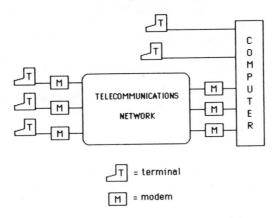

_Π_ = terminal

☐ M = modem

Bit-Oriented
Data-Link Protocols

T HE CHARACTER-ORIENTED DLC PROTOCOLS DISCUSSED IN CHAPTER 11 ALL
have some shortcomings which have been eliminated or greatly reduced by the
development of bit-oriented protocols. The shortcomings include cumbersome techniques for providing data transparency, protocol dependencies on codeset selection,
and the complex hardware and/or software needed to recognize a fairly large set
of control characters and sequences. Unlike the variety of very different character-oriented protocols, there is only one basic bit-oriented protocol scheme in widespread
use today. However there are about a half dozen standards which differ only in some
minor extensions and optional features added to the fundamental operating techniques which are common to all. In this chapter we will concentrate on ISO high-level
data-link control (HDLC), which is generally regarded as the great-grandfather of
the bit-oriented DLC family.

ISO HIGH-LEVEL DATA-LINK CONTROL

The specification of ISO HDLC involves four distinct International Standards—ISO
3309, "Data communication-High-level data-link control procedures-Frame structure"
defines the frame or message structure as the title might suggest. ISO 4335, "Data
communication-High-level data-link control procedures-Elements of procedures"
discusses the HDLC operating modes and defines specific commands and responses.
Two other standards, ISO 6159 and ISO 6256, specify which parts of ISO 4335 apply
to specific operating configurations.

FRAME STRUCTURE

The key to bit-oriented protocols lies in the unique frame structure and delimiting flags which they use. The HDLC frame structure shown in Fig. 12-1 is defined by International Standard ISO 3309 (1979). The flag sequence (01111110) is used to delimit the beginning and end of a message. Whenever it occurs, the flag sequence must be recognized by the receiving station. Once an opening flag is detected, it becomes a simple matter to locate the other fields within the frame. The address field identifies either the destination or source of the message depending upon whether it is a command or a response. The codes for these command and response functions are contained in the control field along with message sequencing numbers. The information field contains the data of interest and can be of any length. To insure that particular data patterns are not mistaken for flags or aborts, *zero-bit insertion/deletion* is used to break up runs of six or more contiguous 1 bits occurring in the data. In the zero-bit insertion scheme, whenever five contiguous 1 bits occur in the address, control, information or FCS fields the transmitter will insert a zero bit after the fifth one, regardless of whether the sixth bit would have been a one or not. This makes life easy on the receiver—whenever it detects five contiguous 1 bits followed by a zero bit it simply deletes the zero bit without regard for the subsequent bits. When the receiver detects six contiguous 1 bits, it must examine the next bit to determine whether it is receiving a flag (01111110) or an abort (01111111). The idle sequence (11111 . . .) can also contain six contiguous 1 bits but it occurs only between messages—not within them. The information field may be omitted in some message formats. The frame check sequence (FCS) is a 16 bit CRC sequence based on the CCITT polynomial which was discussed in Chapter 2. All of the fields in the frame, except for the information field and FCS, are transmitted low-order bit first. The FCS is transmitted high-order bit first. The order of the information field is not specified in the standard and may vary depending upon the particular application of interest.

If a frame is received with an FCS error, the receiving station will discard the entire message and continue as if it had never been received. The frame must be discarded because the error could be located anywhere in the frame making the control field, or even the address, potentially incorrect.

A transmitting station wishing to abort a message may do so by transmitting seven or more contiguous 1 bits while disabling the zero bit insertion process. Upon receiving an abort, a station will discard the aborted message and continue as if it had never been received.

OPERATIONAL MODES

In ISO HDLC documentation the traditional terms "master" and "slave" are replaced by "primary" and "secondary," respectively. A secondary station can operate in either *normal response mode* (NRM) or *asynchronous response mode* (ARM). In NRM operation the secondary may transmit only in response to a request or poll from the primary. The response can consist of one or more messages. In ARM operation the secondary

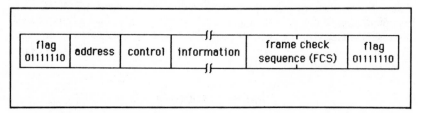

Fig. 12-1. HDLC frame structure.

can transmit without a request from the primary. In all modes a transmitting station must maintain each transmitted message in a buffer until receipt is acknowledged by the receiving station. Acknowledgment of messages is accomplished by means of the sequence numbers contained in the control fields of information (*I format*) and supervisory (*S format*) messages.

CONTROL FIELD

Three different control field formats are defined for either numbered information transfer frames (*I frames*), numbered supervisory frames (*S frames*), or unnumbered control frames (*U frames*) as shown in Fig. 12-2. An extended control field format, as shown in Fig. 12-3, is defined for environments where modulo-8 frame numbering (which permits only 7 unacknowledged frames to be outstanding at any one time) is inadequate. The extended format allows for modulo-128 frame numbering.

POLL/FINAL BIT

The use of the poll/final (P/F) bit in the control field depends on the operating mode and type of station transmitting. A primary station sets the P/F bit in certain command frames (I, RR, REJ, or SREJ) to poll or request a response from a secondary. However, a RNR S command frame sent with the P/F bit set will prohibit the secondary from transmitting I frames. A secondary station operating in normal response mode sets the P/F bit in a response frame to indicate that it is the final frame of the response. The secondary must refrain from further transmission until it is polled again by the primary. In ARM, a secondary sets the P/F bit to indicate that it is responding to a command received from the primary with the P/F bit set.

SEQUENCE NUMBERS

Each station maintains separate modulo-8 counters of messages sent and messages received. Assume that station A transmits a message to station B. When the message is received by B, the send sequence number inserted by A into the control field is compared to station B's received-message counter to determine if any messages from A have been missed. The receive sequence number contained in the received control field is checked to determine the most recent message of B's that is being acknowledged by A. Station B is free to discard the acknowledged message and any earlier ones since it knows from the sequence number that they have been successfully received by A and will not need to be retransmitted.

WATCHDOG TIMERS

To insure that it will not wait forever for a response which may have become garbled or lost in transmission, a primary station must have a *response timer* which is started whenever a command is sent which requires a response. If the response is not received within a certain time interval, the response timer will expire and the primary may initiate recovery procedures. In ARM operation, each secondary must also have a response timer since secondaries can initiate commands which require response from the primary.

INFORMATION FRAMES

Information (I) frames can be sent as commands by the primary and as responses by the secondaries.

1	2	3	4	5	6	7	8
0	LSB	N_S	MSB	P/F	LSB	N_R	MSB

I-frame control field format

1	2	3	4	5	6	7	8
1	0	S	S	P/F	LSB	N_R	MSB

S-frame control field format

1	2	3	4	5	6	7	8
1	1	M	M	P/F	M	M	M

U-frame control field format

N_S = transmitter's send sequence number

N_R = transmitter's receive sequence number

S = supervisory function definition bits

M = control function definition bits

P/F = poll bit in frames from primary
final bit in frames from secondary

Fig. 12-2. HDLC control field formats.

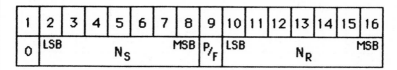

I-frame extended control frame format

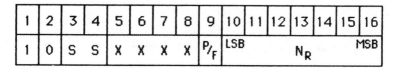

S-frame extended control frame format

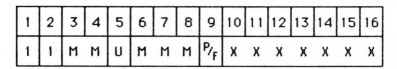

U-frame extended control frame format

N_S = transmitter's send sequence number

N_R = transmitter's receive sequence number

S = supervisory function definition bits

M = control function definition bits

P/F = poll bit in frames from primary
      final bit in frames from secondary

X = Reserved for future use

Fig. 12-3. HDLC extended control field formats.

1	2	3	4	5	6	7	8
1	0	S_3	S_4	P/F	LSB	N_R	MSB

$$\underline{S_3 \quad S_4}$$

S_3	S_4	
0	0	RR – Receive ready
0	1	REJ – Reject
1	0	RNR – Receive not ready
1	1	SREJ – Selective reject

Fig. 12-4. Detailed control field format for HDLC S-frames.

SUPERVISORY FRAMES

The control field in the various supervisory commands and responses will be shown in Fig. 12-4. The two "S" bits are used to indicate the specific type of supervisory frame. Supervisory frames can be either commands from the primary or responses

Table 12-1. HDLC Supervisory Frames.

RR – indicates that sending station is ready to receive information. Also acknowledges receipt of previous I frames.

RNR – indicates that sending station is temporarily unable to receive further I frames.

REJ – requests that receiving station retransmit all recent I frames beginning with frame number NR.

SREJ – requests that receiving station retransmit the single I frame numbered NR.

1	2	3	4	5	6	7	8
1	1	M_3	M_4	P/F	M_6	M_7	M_8

M_3 M_4 M_6 M_7 M_8

M_3	M_4	M_6	M_7	M_8	
0	0	0	0	0	UI – Unnumbered information
0	0	0	0	1	SNRM – Set normal response mode
0	0	0	1	0	DISC – Disconnect
0	0	1	0	0	UP – Unnumbered poll
1	0	0	0	0	SIM – Set initialization mode
1	1	0	0	0	SARM – Set asynchronous response mode
1	1	0	1	0	SARME – Set async. response mode extended
1	1	0	1	1	SNRME – Set normal response mode extended
1	1	1	0	1	XID – Exchange identification

Fig. 12-5. Detailed control field format for HDLC U-frame commands.

from the secondaries. *Receive ready* (RR) is used by a station to indicate that it is ready to receive information and to acknowledge receipt of I frames up through sequence number $N_R - 1$. *Receive not ready* (RNR) is used by a station to indicate that it is temporarily unable to receive further I frames due to lack of buffer space or any other reason. Reject (REJ) is used to request retransmission of all I frames beginning with frame number N_R. On the other hand, selective reject (SREJ) is used to request transmission of the single I frame numbered N_R. The various supervisory frames are summarized in Table 12-1.

UNNUMBERED COMMANDS AND RESPONSES

The control field in *unnumbered commands* will be as shown in Fig. 12-5. The five

Table 12-2. HDLC Unnumbered Commands.

UI – used by primary station to send information to secondaries without involving any of the sequence numbering mechanisms.

SNRM – directs the receiving secondary to operate in normal response mode.

DISC – directs the receiving secondary to logically disconnect itself from the network.

UP – used by primary station to poll secondaries without involving any of the sequence numbering mechanisms.

SIM – directs the receiving secondary to initialize its link level control functions.

SARM – directs the receiving secondary to operate in the asynchronous response mode.

SARME – directs the receiving secondary to operate in the extended asynchronous response mode.

SNRME – directs the receiving secondary to operate in the extended normal response mode.

XID – identifies the primary and directs the receiving secondary to identify itself in a response

1	2	3	4	5	6	7	8
1	1	M_3	M_4	P/F	M_6	M_7	M_8

M_3 M_4 M_6 M_7 M_8

M_3	M_4	M_6	M_7	M_8	
0	0	0	0	0	UI – Unnumbered information
0	0	0	1	0	RD – Request disconnect
0	0	1	1	0	UA – Unnumbered acknowledge
1	0	0	0	0	RIM – Request initialization mode
1	0	0	0	1	CMDR – Command reject
1	1	0	0	0	DM – Disconnect mode
1	1	1	0	1	XID – Exchange identification

Fig. 12-6. Detailed control field format for HDLC U-frame responses.

"M" bits are used as indicated to indicate the specific type of command. The major use of each command is listed in Table 12-2. The control field for *unnumbered responses* is shown in Fig. 12-6, and the major use of each response is listed in Table 12-3.

SYSTEM CONFIGURATIONS

In *unbalanced configurations* the roles of primary and secondary reside in distinct stations as shown in Fig. 12-7, while in *balanced configurations* the roles of primary and secondary reside together in *combined stations* as shown in Fig. 12-8. Different elements of ISO 4335 are used for balanced and unbalanced operation. ISO 6159 and ISO 6256 define the applicable elements for unbalanced and balanced operation, respectively.

Table 12-3. HDLC Unnumbered Responses.

UI – used by a secondary station to send information to the primary without involving any of the sequence numbering mechanisms.

RD – requests permission from the primary for the sending station to logically disconnect itself.

UA – used by a secondary station to acknowledge unnumbered commands received from the primary.

RIM – indicates that the sending secondary station needs to initialize its link level control functions.

CMDR – indicates that the sending secondary is unable to accept a previous command from the primary because the command is invalid, the secondary has insufficient available buffer area, or the received command message is out of sequence.

DM – reports status of a responding secondary which is logically disconnected.

XID – identifies the sending secondary that is responding to an **XID** command from the primary.

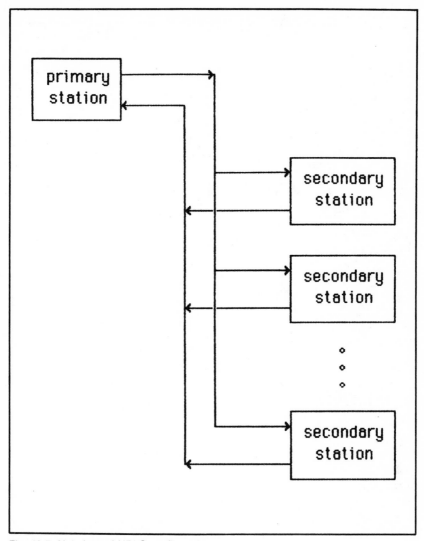

Fig. 12-7. Unbalanced HDLC configuration.

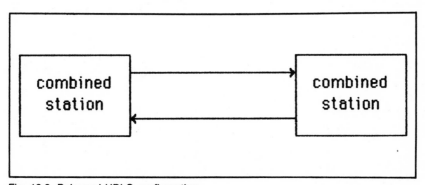

Fig. 12-8. Balanced HDLC configuration.

Chapter 13

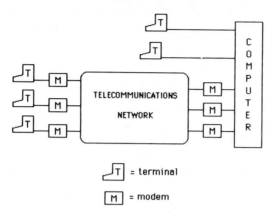

$\boxed{\!{\sqrt{\!\!\,T}}}$ = terminal

$\boxed{M}$ = modem

Local Area Networks

A S WE HAVE SEEN IN PREVIOUS CHAPTERS, MODEMS AND PHONE LINES WORK well together for linking a variety of computing machines dispersed across a continent, and a simple serial interface is fine for connecting a computer and a limited number of peripherals in close proximity. There are numerous midsized installations, however, which call for something slightly different. Applications, such as linking together all the intelligent machines in a large office building or college campus, are often best served by *local area network* (LAN) technology. In this chapter we will look in general at network accessing schemes and various LAN topologies; while in Chapter 14 we take a more detailed look at the Xerox Ethernet, which is a tremendously popular standard for office environment networking. Then in Chapter 15 we will survey the most popular propriety LANs and look at the wide scope of standardization efforts being attempted by the IEEE 802 series of LAN specifications.

LAN FEATURES

The major commercial uses of local area networks are information exchange and resource sharing between intelligent machines in the workplace. To effectively accomplish these ends, LANs should possess the following attributes:

- high speed and bandwidth sufficient to meet data throughput requirements
- reliability and maintainability
- low cost
- compatibility with a large variety of connected equipments
- flexibility and expandibility
- easy to use

When making tradeoffs in the design and selection of LAN schemes, a major guideline is provided by the fact that 80 percent of the information generated within a particular department is used entirely within the department, while only 20 percent comes from or goes to outside offices. Thus primary consideration should be given to communications within a department, with links to the outside relegated to a secondary level of concern.

DIGITAL SWITCHING

Imagine having a pair of wires between your telephone and every other telephone in the world—clearly a ridiculous arrangement! Instead, as discussed in Chapter 5, your phone is connected to a central office which contains switches for connecting your line to other local lines or to trunks connected to distant switching centers or central offices. The telephone network employs a *circuit switching* scheme in which the various switches in the network act to establish a circuit connection between the calling phone and the called phone. The circuit thus established is maintained for the duration of the call. Circuit switching can also be used for data traffic, and in fact it is used whenever data is transmitted by modems connected into the public dialup telephone network. However this usage is by default rather than by choice— the public telephone network already exists and it is usually the most convenient way to connect geographically separated locations without incurring large capital expenses. When a dedicated network is to be installed or leased, there are other switching techniques which can be used to take advantage of the bursty nature of data transmissions and use the network resources more efficiently. Most of the older data networks such as telegraphy and military communications systems employ a *message switching* scheme in which the complete data message is transmitted to a switching center where it is stored until the necessary links become available to forward the message to either its final destination or to the next switching center along the way. While message switching makes efficient use of the network links, messages can spend minutes or even hours in storage at a switching center while waiting for a heavily used link to become available. Any kind of realtime query-and-response or interactive session becomes difficult if not impossible. A third major digital switching technique is *packet switching*, which combines some aspects of both message and circuit switching. In packet switching, the data traffic is broken up into short packets of approximately 100 to 2000 bits each. These packets are then sent using the same store-and-forward technique used in message switching; but since the packets are short the delays are short, and near realtime performance becomes possible. When the distances spanned by the network are relatively short and when there is a need for fine-grained and flexible incremental growths in many LANs, none of the three traditional switching techniques is completely adequate. Therefore some new switching techniques have been developed specifically for the LAN environment. These techniques incorporate some aspects of message, circuit, and packet switching along with some new elements.

NETWORK TOPOLOGY

The simplest way to connect two stations is with a direct point-to-point link between them. A network containing several nodes can be interconnected by placing a point-to-point link between each pair of nodes as shown in Fig. 13-1. This structure is sometimes called a *fully connected mesh*, and requires $N \times (N-1)$ links in a network of N nodes. As the number of nodes gets large, the number of point-to-point links

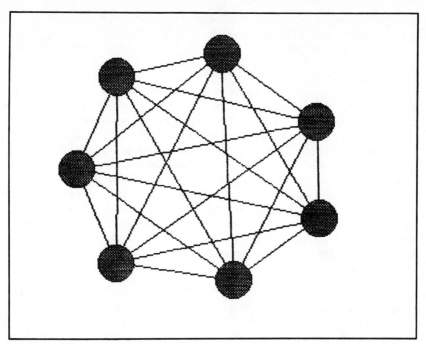

Fig. 13-1. Fully connected mesh network.

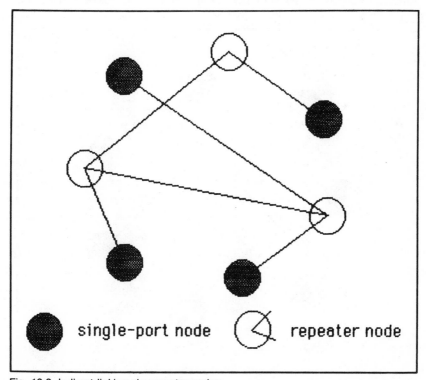

single-port node ⟨ repeater node

Fig. 13-2. Indirect linking via repeater nodes.

gets unwieldy and the fully connected mesh becomes an unsuitable approach. There are two alternatives for reducing the number of links. Some pairs of stations can be connected indirectly through other stations, as shown in Fig. 13-2, rather than directly through point-to-point links, or *multidrop* links can be used as shown in Fig. 13-3. The indirect linking approach of Fig. 13-2 requires that the intermediate nodes be *routing nodes* capable of processing routing information contained in the messages and acting appropriately to forward the messages onto the proper links for approaching their final destination nodes. The multidrop approach eliminates the need for routing nodes but introduces the need for controlling transmit access to the link to insure that different stations do not attempt to transmit simultaneously, thereby creating a conflict or *contention* on the link. Figure 13-4 illustrates the type of unconstrained network structure which can be formed by arbitrarily combining both point-to-point and multipoint links together with routing and nonrouting nodes. Although some networks of this type exist, more efficient and manageable networks can be created if the network structure or *topology* is constrained to a particular form such as a *star, ring, tree* or *bus*. Each particular topology has its own advantages and disadvantages and each works best with different access control and routing schemes.

STAR TOPOLOGY

A star topology is a natural choice for a LAN in which communications control functions are centralized in a single node or hub as shown in Fig. 13-5. In most operating protocols, the outlying nodes may transmit only in response to a poll or message from the hub. Since the hub is involved in every message transaction, the star structure works best when most communications are between an outlying nodes and the cen-

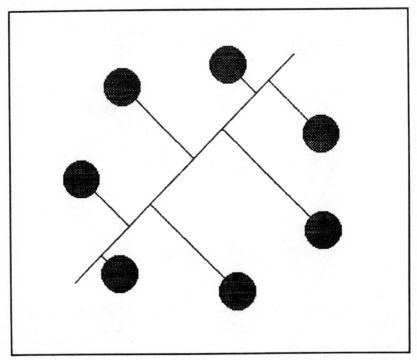

Fig. 13-3. Multidrop link.

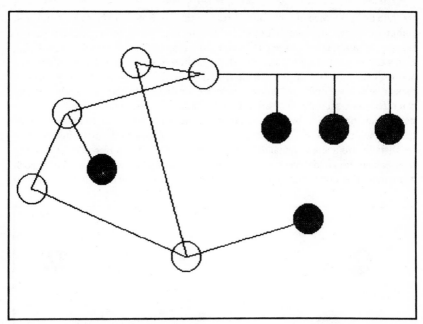

Fig. 13-4. Unconstrained network structure.

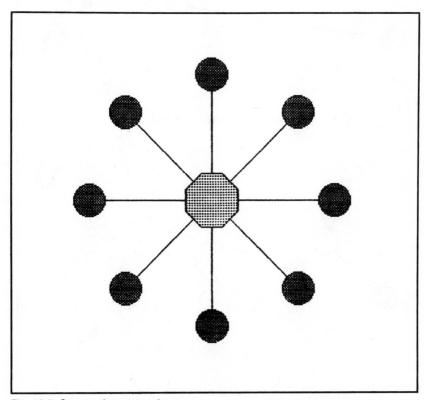

Fig. 13-5. Star topology network.

tral hub as in the case of a number of remote terminals networked to a central host computer. A star topology, however, can still be used for node-to-node communications which are relayed by the hub. A star has a major advantage in that the outlying nodes can be connected to the network through very simple interfaces without any address recognition or repeater circuitry, since the nodes can assume that any message appearing on their dedicated link was intended for them. Furthermore, a star topology can offer some security since all communications between nodes are subject to approval and supervision by the hub. However, the star does suffer from some shortcomings which make it unacceptable for certain applications. In many installations the distance from one terminal to the next may be relatively short, while the distance from each terminal to the central hub is relatively long as shown in Fig. 13-6. In such a situation, the total cabling required to connect each terminal directly to the central

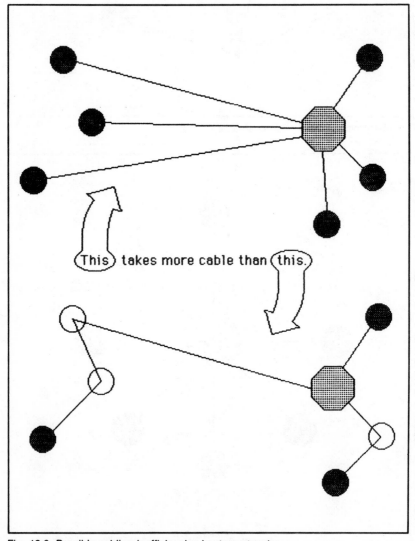

Fig. 13-6. Possible cabling inefficiencies in star networks.

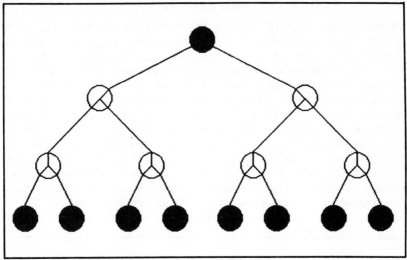

Fig. 13-7. Tree topology network.

node would be significantly greater than the cabling required if some of the terminals were connected indirectly through other terminals as is done in some other topologies. Using nodes as repeaters for indirect connections can save on cabling, but the nodes then need to be equipped with a means for separating messages for themselves from those which are only to be repeated for other nodes. The system designer must decide which is the more economical approach—abundant cabling with relatively simple node interfaces or less cabling with more complex nodes equipped to recognize addresses and repeat messages. Another shortcoming of star topologies is that they require relatively complex center hub node equipment, which can cripple the entire network with just a single failure.

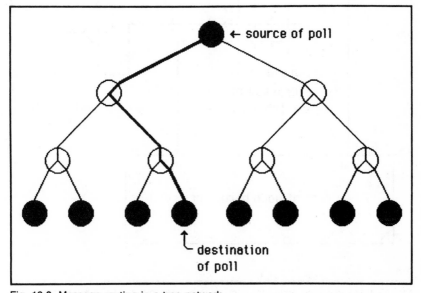

← source of poll

destination of poll

Fig. 13-8. Message routing in a tree network.

155

TREE TOPOLOGY

The tree topology shown in Fig. 13-7 can be viewed as an improved star type system in which cabling requirements are reduced by using repeater nodes to relay messages to and from other nodes. Just as with the star topology, a centralized polling scheme works well in a tree with control functions centralized in the root node. Other channel allocation and access control schemes can be used, but things could get a bit tricky. Consider a polling message which must be routed from the route node to one of the branch nodes as shown in Fig. 13-8. Each intermediate node must somehow decide on which branch the message should be repeated in order to reach its final destination. In the simplest method, called *flooding*, each intermediate node repeats each received message onto all of its outbound branch links. When the intended destination node recognizes its own address, it will accept the message and formulate a reply. The reply will be sent via the node's outbound trunk link back towards the root node. The intermediate node which receives this will not know beforehand on which inbound branch link the response will appear since it relayed the original poll out on

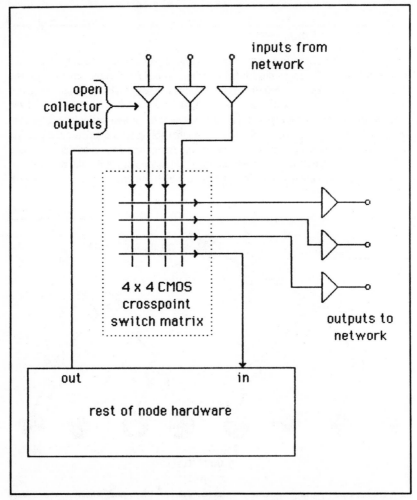

Fig. 13-9. I/O switching matrix for interfacing a node to the links in a tree network.

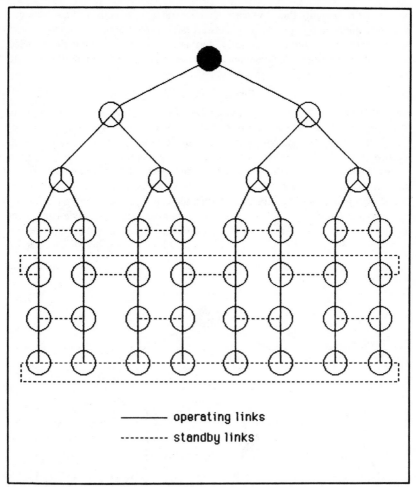

Fig. 13-10. Reconfigurable tree network.

all branches not knowing which one was really aimed at the destination node. Rather than attempting to locate the link bearing the reply activity, the node can just logically OR together the activity on all of the inbound branch links. Of course this will require that all inactive links be held at logical zero. As in all topologies involving repeater nodes, the failure of a repeater can cripple all or part of the network. The usual countermeasures include robust, highly reliable repeater designs which "never" fail, failsafe bypassing circuits to automatically bypass failed repeaters, or extra links which can be used to establish alternate paths to all functioning nodes after a repeater fails. The tree topology is particularly well suited for this last approach. Since some types of repeater failure can cause continuous garbage to be output, the nodes must be designed to allow selective disabling of the branch inputs so that valid reply activity will not have to be ORed together with garbage activity. A simple I/O switching matrix to accomplish this is shown in Fig. 13-9. If each node in a tree is equipped with such a matrix and a few extra links are added to the network, the resulting reconfigurable system, shown in Fig. 13-10, will endure single node failures and still communicate with all nodes except for the failed one. The nodes adjacent to the failed one simply reconfigure their I/O matrices to isolate it from the rest of the network, and other nodes reconfigure to connect the stranded piece of the branch to the end of another branch as shown in Fig. 13-11. Furthermore, each node within the stranded section must reconfigure to accommodate connection to the root via a different link.

RING TOPOLOGY

An example of ring topology is shown in Fig. 13-12. Each node is connected to its neighbor on either side by a point-to-point link, and each node's interface must participate in message routing only to the extent of either accepting or forwarding each message received. The interface hardware is relatively simple but it is usually designed for very high reliability so that messages can be forwarded even if other parts of the node should fail. In order to attain both reliability and maximum flexibility in selection of equipment, the interface transceivers and control logic are often placed in a *ring interface unit* (RIU), which is separated from the rest of the node equipment as shown in Fig. 13-13. Thus, potentially unreliable terminals and peripherals can be safely connected to the network just so long as high-quality, well-designed RIUs

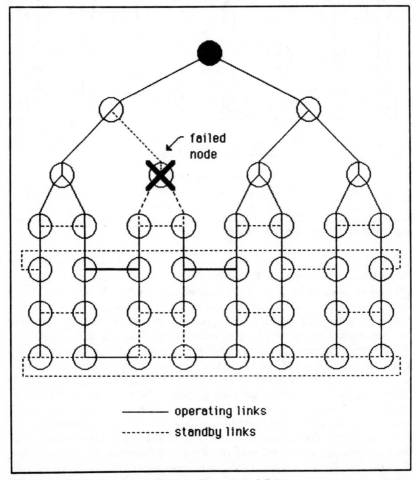

Fig. 13-11. Tree network reconfigured after a node failure.

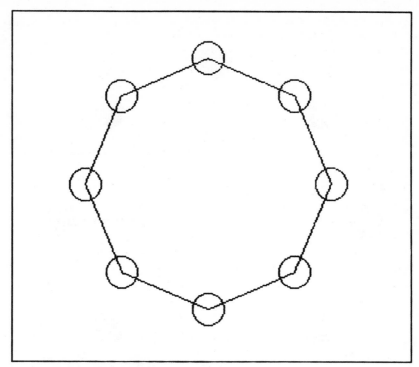

Fig. 13-12. Ring topology network.

are used. Unlike the star, the ring topology usually has no centralized control node, so alternative means must be provided to regulate transmissions of the nodes and prevent contention and message collisions. The two most popular ring-based schemes are *token passing rings* and *slotted rings*.

TOKEN PASSING

In networks with a ring topology, *token passing* is a popular technique for controlling access to the network transmission medium. An *idle token*, consisting of a unique bit pattern, is circulated from node to node around the ring. When the idle token is received by a node which has data to be transmitted, the node changes it into a *busy token* before relaying it on to the next node followed immediately by a packet or message containing data. The busy token and data packet travel around the ring and each node examines the addressing information in the packet in order to determine if the packet should be accepted as input or merely relayed on to the next node. When the packet has traversed the complete ring and returns to the node which originated it, the node will remove the packet from the network by opting not to repeat it for the next node. The originating node will also replace the busy token with an idle token which circulates until some node again has data to be transmitted. Since the originating node receives its own data after it has traversed the entire ring, the node can compare the received message to the transmitted message and easily determine if any errors have been introduced during transmission.

One disadvantage of this scheme is that each message ties up the network during the entire time needed to completely traverse the ring and return to the originating node. If the messages are short and the ring propagation time is relatively long, this

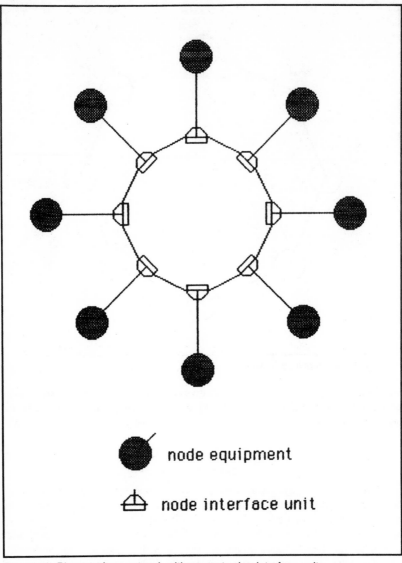

node equipment

node interface unit

Fig. 13-13. Ring topology network with separate ring interface units.

can result in very inefficient use of the link capacity. This problem can be mitigated by using a *multiple token* scheme in which the originating node appends a new idle token onto the end of its data transmission thus allowing other nodes to add messages behind the first message without having to wait for the first message to completely circle the ring. Ensuring that the token patterns remain unique is a problem which can be approached from either a character-oriented or bit-oriented viewpoint. As in the case of character-oriented data-link protocols, the character set used for data can be restricted so that a pattern in the data will never be mistaken for a token. Situations which require data transparency can be handled by escape sequence techniques discussed in Chapter 11. Although the character-oriented approach will work, the bit-oriented techniques discussed in Chapter 12 will be much less cumbersome and are usually preferred. One major problem associated with some token passing schemes is the relative difficulty of recovery and reconstructing a new token whenever an idle token is lost due to a node failure or noise disturbance.

SLOTTED RINGS

In the *slotted ring* approach a number of tokens separated by fixed-length slots for data packets continuously circulate around the ring. When a node has data to be transmitted, it sets the slot status to busy and inserts the data packet into the slot. Such a scheme can be operated in a frame-synchronous fashion thus eliminating the need for complex token recognition hardware.

BUS TOPOLOGY

Figure 13-14 illustrates the *lineal bus* topology that is conceptually very simple. The output drivers and input receivers of every node are directly connected to the interconnecting media or bus. Although it may appear that the ends of a bus can be joined together to form a ring, this is usually not the case. As conventionally defined, rings involve point to point links with active repeaters at each node, while a bus is usually a multidrop scheme in which messages are broadcast to all stations connected to the bus. In order to distinguish between messages to be accepted as input and those messages to be ignored, each node must be capable of recognizing its own address whenever it is included in a message. Access to the bus can be controlled by token passing schemes similar to those used in ring topologies. However, due to the multidrop nature of the bus, the tokens must be addressed to facilitate passing them to a specific node. An alternative scheme is *carrier-sense multiple access with collision detection* (CSMA/CD), which is used in the Ethernet™ network and discussed in Chapter 14. A major shortcoming of the multidrop bus architecture is that a failure in the bus interface of a single node can "hang" the bus thereby disabling the entire network.

BROADBAND LAN TECHNIQUES

So far all the techniques discussed in this chapter have been *baseband* techniques that assume that only one transmitting station at a time can use any particular cable link.

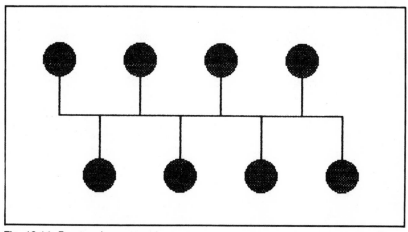

Fig. 13-14. Bus topology network.

Any sharing of the link is accomplished in a time-division fashion. *Broadband LANs* are an alternative approach in which links can share in a frequency-division fashion. In their simplest form, broadband LANs are just baseband LANs to which modems have been added for interfacing each node to the physical transmission media. While these modems may at first appear to be an unnecessary extravagance, they can bring to the LAN all the same advantages that they bring to the telecommunications environment—better performance in spite of noisy, lossy, or distorting media. This can be a necessity in LANs which span relatively large distances or that must make use of an installed base of inferior cabling. The broadband approach is even more attractive when relatively wideband channels are needed or when FDM (frequency-division multiplexing) techniques are used to fit a large number of narrower channels into the wide bandwidths available on media such as coaxial and fiber optic cables. By modulating the baseband signals into different frequency bands, several different LAN systems and even video can be combined together and carried simultaneously on the same media. There is very little specialized hardware expressly for broadband LAN usage. Most of the systems in use today use devices such as filters, mixers, splitters, modulators and demodulators which were originally developed for FDM or cable TV use. Although Wangnet is an example to the contrary, most LANs currently operating in the small office environment are of the baseband type, but this may change as teleconferencing and other video applications grow in importance. The wide bandwidths of full-motion video signals makes them virtually unsupportable with baseband LAN techniques.

THE ALOHA NETWORK

LANs are not limited to just wireline implementations; in fact, one of the early LANs was the ALOHA radio network developed at the University of Hawaii in the late sixties and early seventies. This system uses two uhf radio channels at 407.350 MHz and 413.475 MHz (with a 100 kHz bandwidth) to link together several computers and a number of terminals scattered throughout the Hawaiian Islands.

Chapter 14

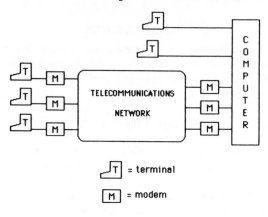

$\boxed{\text{T}}$ = terminal

$\boxed{\text{M}}$ = modem

Ethernet

E THERNET IS A PHYSICAL AND LINK LAYER LAN STANDARD DEVELOPED AT THE Xerox Palo Alto Research Center (PARC) by Robert M. Metcalfe, David Boggs, Bulter W. Lampson, and Charles P. Thacker. Originally conceived as a means for linking together a number of experimental Alto computers being developed at PARC, Ethernet has grown into a major contender in the office LAN arena. Primarily due to the evangelistic efforts of Metcalfe, Ethernet is now supported by a tripartite consortium of Xerox, Intel, and Digital Equipment Corporation. Certain features of Ethernet are protected by Xerox patents and developers of Ethernet products may obtain licensing information from Xerox Corporation, Director of Licensing, Long Ridge Road, Stamford, CT 06904.

DESIGN PHILOSOPHY

A number of alleged design goals for Ethernet are listed in version 1.0 of the specification. These goals include simplicity, low cost, compatibility between all implementations of Ethernet, addressing flexibility, high speed, low delays, stable behavior of the network under all traffic loading conditions, and maintainability. I say "alleged" goals because a great deal of controversy still exists concerning how well these goals have been met—particularly in the area of economics. The particular choice of cabling and station connection hardware has proven to be so expensive that an alternative, Ethernet-like standard, dubbed Cheapernet, has been developed that uses cheaper cabling and connections. (Presently an Ethernet transceiver alone costs about $300—the controller and cabling are extra!) Items which the Ethernet standard specifically lists as non-goals include full duplex operation, error control beyond simple detection of bit errors in the physical channel, built-in security features, variable operating speeds, prioritization of station access to the channel, and protection against hostile users operating in the network.

PHYSICAL LAYER

Compatibility among devices made by different manufacturers is a major goal of the Ethernet design. To insure such compatibility, the physical layer specifications are rather complete and inflexible. The physical layer channel hardware performs the following functions:

1. Transfers serial bit stream from the data link layer to the physical media and vice versa.

2. Generates the clock used for synchronization and timing operations.

3. Detects collisions between simultaneous transmissions from two or more stations.

4. Detects the presence of a carrier signal on the media.

5 Encodes and decodes the Manchester line code transmitted between stations. (See Chapter 2 for a discussion of Manchester line coding.)

6. Generates a preamble sequence used to synchronize all channel elements before each frame is transmitted.

The major components of an Ethernet station are shown in Fig. 14-1. Physical separation of the coax transceiver from the rest of the station is optional, but it will be necessary in most installations since the transceiver must be located within a few centimeters of the coax in order to comply with capacitive loading limitations. Since it will often be impractical to locate the entire station within centimeters of the coax, the Ethernet specification includes a standard interface and cable configuration for remoting the transceiver from the rest of the station hardware.

COAXIAL CABLE CONFIGURATION

The configuration for a typical Ethernet system is shown in Fig. 14-2. A number of stations can be connected to a single segment of coax, and repeaters can be used

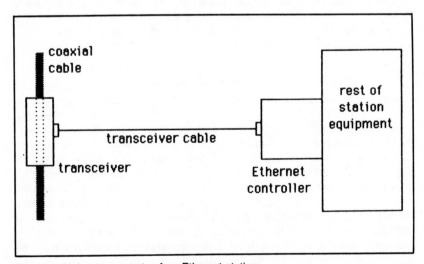

Fig. 14-1. Major components of an Ethernet station.

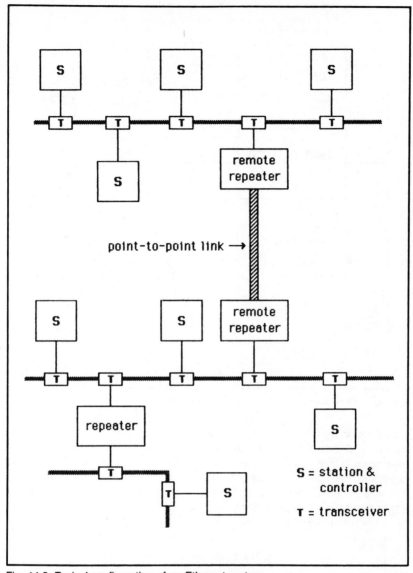

Fig. 14-2. Typical configuration of an Ethernet system.

to link together different cable segments. The specification permits up to 500 meters of coax in each segment and up to two repeaters in a path between any two stations. A total of 100 transceivers and repeaters may be connected to each segment. In addition to the segment cabling, up to 1000 meters of point-to-point cabling can be used between repeaters to link together separately located segments. Each station can be linked to its transceiver through a transceiver cable measuring up to 50 meters in length.

CHANNEL ACCESS MANAGEMENT

For channel allocation and contention resolution, Ethernet uses a scheme called *carrier-*

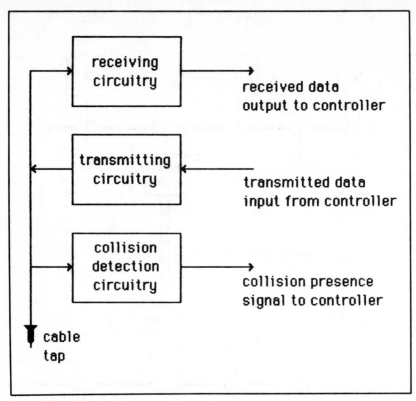

Fig. 14-3. Block diagram of an Ethernet transceiver.

sense multiple-access with collision detection (CSMA/CD). In this scheme, the receiving section of each station continuously monitors activity on the coaxial cable to determine when it may permit the transmitting section to transmit data. If activity is detected on the channel, the transmitter must defer transmission. After the coax has been idle for at least 9.6 μsec, the transmitter is allowed to transmit a message if it has one pending. This procedure will reduce, but not eliminate, the chance of contention between two or more stations attempting to transmit at the same time.

COLLISION DETECTION

If two stations do attempt to transmit at the same time, their messages will produce a *collision* that can be detected by the transceiver. If a collision is detected at a transmitting station, the station will continue to transmit for 32 to 48 bits and then stop. The continued transmission after collision detection is called a *jam* and is performed to insure that all stations are able to detect the collision. Very short collisions of only a few bits may not be detectable at all locations in the network due to the bit patterns and relative phasing between the colliding signals. Extending a collision to last for at least 32 bits virtually guarantees that it will be detectable by all stations.

BACKOFF AND RETRANSMISSION

After transmission is stopped because of a collision, the station will wait or backoff for a random (but constrained) time interval before attempting to retransmit the frame.

166

The random delay is intended to prevent the contending stations from simultaneously attempting a retransmission that would result in a second collision. The backoff delay, D, for the n-th retransmission attempt is given by:

$$D = (r)(51.2 \ \mu sec)$$

where r is a uniformly distributed random integer in the range $0 < r < 2^k$ with k = min(n,10). Selecting a backoff delay this way will tend to increase the delay for subsequent retransmission attempts. The standard points out that this is the "most aggressive" retransmission behavior that a station may exhibit, but that a station is free to introduce additional delays beyond those specified.

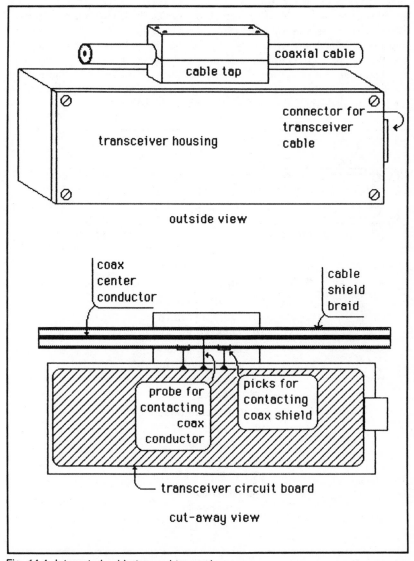

Fig. 14-4. Integrated cable tap and transceiver.

TRANSCEIVER

Figure 14-3 is a functional block diagram of an Ethernet transceiver. In order to successfully connect up to 100 stations to each segment of cable, the electrical characteristics of the "coax-side" of each transceiver must be carefully designed to minimize capacitive loading and signal reflections on the cable. The high reactance due to the 10 Mbps signal present on the coax requires that a rather low limit of 2 picofarads be imposed on the maximum shunt capacitance of the cable-to-transceiver connection. At present, locating the transceiver within about 3 centimeters of the coax is the only practical way to meet the capacitance limitations imposed by the standard. This obviously dictates that the physical connection to the coax must be an integral part of the transceiver. Figure 14-4 shows the mechanical aspects of an integrated cable tap and transceiver housing design, which is typical of commercially available units. In addition to low capacitive loading, the transceiver must present a dc input shunt resistance of at least 50k ohms. When the transceiver is not transmitting, the collision detection circuitry must indicate the presence of a collision whenever the average signal power on the coax exceeds the worst case power which could be produced by two other transceiver outputs. When the transceiver is transmitting, a collision must be indicated whenever the average signal power on the cable exceeds the highest level which the transceiver could produce by itself.

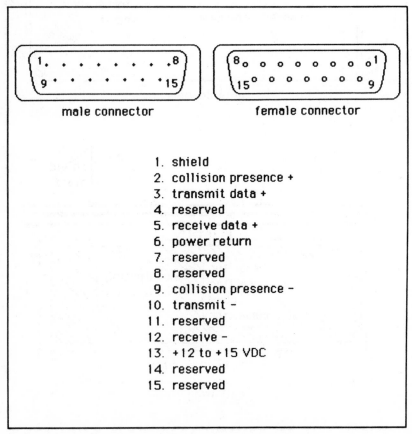

Fig. 14-5. Pin assignments for an Ethernet transceiver cable.

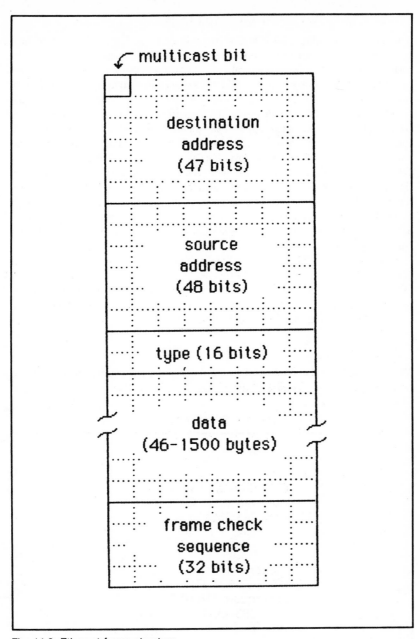

Fig. 14-6. Ethernet frame structure.

TRANSCEIVER CABLE AND INTERFACE

The transceiver cable connects the transceiver to a separately located Ethernet controller. The transceiver end of the cable must have a female 15 pin subminiature "D" connector and the controller end must have a male of the same type. The pin assignments for these connectors are shown in Fig. 14-5. Manchester encoding/decoding of the transmit and receive signals is performed by the controller.

FRAME STRUCTURE

The internal structure of an Ethernet frame is shown in Fig. 14-6. The first field transmitted is the destination address field which is 6 bytes long. The first bit of the address is either set to zero to indicate the physical address of an individual station or set to one to indicate a multicast address assigned to a group of stations. The remaining 47 bits constitute an address that is unique for each Ethernet station in the world. (Forty-seven bits provide over 140 trillion different addresses, so Ethernet will be ancient history long before any addresses need to be reused.) To insure that address assignments remain unique, blocks of addresses are allocated by: Xerox Corporation, Ethernet Address Administration Office, 3333 Coyote Hill Road, Palo Alto, CA 94304. The source address is not interpreted at the data-link layer, but its location in the frame is specified to facilitate standardized interfacing to higher-level protocols that do make use of its contents. Likewise, the type field, which indicates which higher level protocol is to be used to interpret the frame contents, is not interpreted at the data-link layer. Type field codes are also unique and assigned by the Ethernet Address Administration Office.

The data field is fully transparent and no particulars concerning its content are specified by Ethernet. The minimum and maximum length limits are specified however, and the values of these limits are a direct result of physical layer considerations to be discussed later in this chapter. The FCS field contains a 32-bit CRC value, which is calculated by the method discussed in Chapter 2.

FRAME RECEPTION

The data-link layer of a receiving station will recognize the beginning of an incoming frame based on a carrier-sense notification from the physical layer. If the destination

Table 14-1. Ethernet Vendors.

3Com
1390 Shorebird Way
Mountain View, CA 94043
(415) 961-9602

Interlan
155 Swanson Rd.
Oxborough, MA 01719
(617) 263-9929

Ungermann-Bass, Inc.
2560 Mission College Blvd
Santa Clara, CA 95050
(408) 496-0111

address indicates that the frame is intended for the station, the station will accept the frame and compute its CRC value. If the received frame does not contain an integer number of bytes or if it exhibits a CRC error, an error condition is reported to higher level protocols for subsequent recovery actions. Since valid frames will always contain at least 64 bytes, a received frame containing less than 64 bytes will be assumed to be a fragment resulting from a collision and will be discarded.

ETHERNET VENDORS

Table 14-1 lists three leading vendors of Ethernet products for personal computers.

Chapter 15

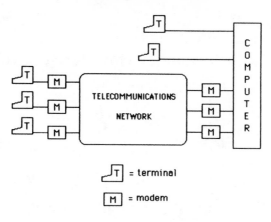

$\boxed{\text{J}\text{T}}$ = terminal

$\boxed{\text{M}}$ = modem

IEEE 488/GPIB

A BOUT FIFTEEN YEARS AGO, A VARIETY OF TEST EQUIPMENT AND INSTRUMEN-
tation packages began to appear equipped with digital interfaces to permit setup
and operation of the equipment under computer control. In 1972 Hewlett-Packard
introduced the *Hewlett-Packard Interface BUS* (HP-IB), which was a standardized interface configuration and operating protocol for all HP equipment supplied with digital
control interfaces. After some modification, the HP-IB was adopted by the IEEE in
1975 as IEEE Standard 488-1975 "Digital Interface for Programmable Instrumentation." After some primarily editorial and cosmetic changes, the standard was published
again in 1978 as *IEEE Standard 499-1978.* This is also referred to as the *General
Purpose Interface Bus* (GPIB). Although called a "bus" or an "interface," IEEE Std
488 really defines the physical layer and data-link control layer of a local area network for digital communications between computers and various pieces of instrumentation and laboratory equipment.

GPIB OVERVIEW

A typical GPIB network is shown in Fig. 15-1. The various stations are each connected to three busses—the *data bus, data byte transfer control bus,* and *general interface management bus.* The signal lines in these busses are discussed in the sections
below and summarized in Table 15-1. The stations of the network can exhibit three
different types of operation—*talker, listener,* and *controller. Talkers* transmit data and
listeners receive data. However, all data transfers must be orchestrated by a *controller.* The controller must address both the talker that is to transmit and the listeners
that are to receive it. Note that talker, listener, and controller capabilities may occur individually or in any combination within each station.

Table 15-1. GPIB Signal Lines.

Data Bus

DIO1   least significant data bit
DIO2
DIO3
DIO4
DIO5
DIO6
DIO7
DIO8   most significant data bit

Data Byte Transfer Control Bus

NRFD   not ready for data
DAV   data valid
NDAC   not data accepted

General Interface Management Bus

IFC   interface clear
ATN   attention
EOI   end or identify
REN   remote enable
SRQ   service request

DATA BUS

The *data bus* carries both station-to-station messages and certain interface messages. The bus contains eight bidirectional signal lines that carry messages in an asynchronous bit-parallel byte-serial format.

DATA BYTE TRANSFER CONTROL BUS

The *data byte transfer control bus* consists of three signal lines that are used to perform the handshaking required to transfer bytes on the data bus. The *not ready for data* (NRFD) line is asserted by any listener that is not ready to receive data. A potential talker may not proceed until it senses that all listeners have de-asserted NRFD. After placing its data onto the data bus, the talker will wait until the lines have settled and then it will assert the *data valid* (DAV) line. Upon sensing the change in DAV, all active listeners will assert NRFD to indicate that they are not ready for additional

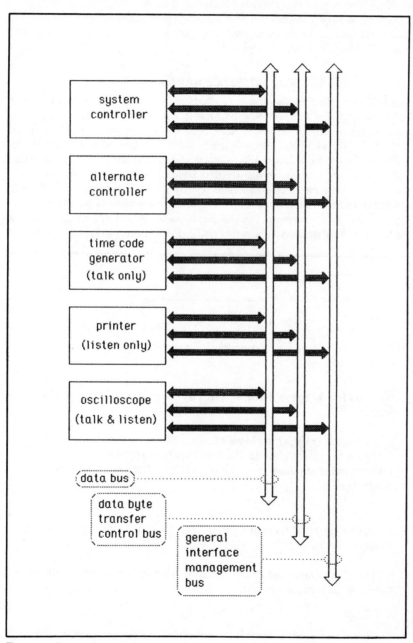

Fig. 15-1. Typical GPIB signal lines.

data. After each listener reads the data it will de-assert the *not data accepted* (NDAC) line to indicate that it has accepted the data. After the talker senses that all listeners have de-asserted NDAC it will de-assert DAV and prepare to transmit the next byte. Upon sensing that DAV has become false, the listeners will each assert NDAC.

Readers should be aware that IEEE 488 calls attention to the fact that this three-wire handshake is claimed to be covered by a patent owned by Hewlett-Packard. The standard further notes that Hewlett-Packard has indicated their willingness to grant a license to use these patents "on reasonable and nondiscriminatory terms and conditions." Details can be obtained from the Hewlett-Packard legal department at 1501 Page Mill Road, Palo Alto, CA 94304.

GENERAL INTERFACE MANAGEMENT BUS

The *general interface management bus* consists of five signal lines—IFC, ATN, SRQ, REN, and EOI. The *interface clear* (IFC) line is asserted by the system controller to force the entire network into a reset state. A number of controllers can be connected to the bus at the same time, but only one of these is designated as the system controller and permitted to assert IFC. The *attention* (ATN) line is asserted by a controller to indicate that it is driving the data bus and hence that the contents of the data bus are to be interpreted as a command from the controller. A controller will assert both ATN and the *end or identify* (EOI) line to perform a *parallel polling* of other stations on the network. The EOI line alone is asserted by a talker to indicate the last byte of a data block. The *remote enable* (REN) line is asserted by a controller

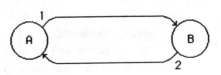

(A)- **device trigger idle state (DTIS)**--The DT function is inactive.

(B)- **device trigger active state (DTAC)**--The DT function issues a trigger signal to the local instrumentation. The instrumentation uses this signal to cause the start of normal operation.

1. Upon command from the controller, a station's DT function will exit (A) and enter (B).

2. When the command from the controller is de-asserted, the DT function will return to (A).

Fig. 15-2. State diagram of the GPIB device trigger (DT) function.

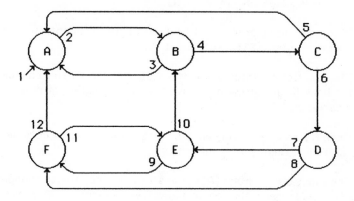

(A) **source idle state (SIDS)**--The SH function is not active.

(B) **source generate state (SGNS)**--The local instrumentation is generating a new message byte and the SH function is waiting for it.

(C) **source delay state (SDYS)**--The SH function is waiting for the signal lines of the data bus to settle and for all the acceptor stations to become ready for new data. During this state the station is not permitted to change the contents of the data byte on the bus.

(D) **source transfer state (STRS)**--The data bus is held steady, and the SH function asserts the DAV line. During this state the station is not permitted to change the contents of the data byte on the bus.

(E) **source wait for new cycle state (SWNS)**--The SH function requests the local instrumentation to place the next data byte on the bus and then waits for a new data transfer to start. The DAV line should be de-asserted either sometime during this state or upon transition into any other state.

(F) **source idle wait state (SIWS)**--The external aspects of the SH function are not active, but internally the function continues to wait for the start of a new data transfer cycle.

Fig. 15-3. State diagram of the GPIB source handshake (SH) function.

1. The SH function powers up in (A).

2. If the station is providing a new data byte to the interface, the SH function enters (B) to wait for it.

3. The function re-enters (A) if the status of the station changes and it is no longer either an active talker, controller, or responder to a serial poll.

4. Once the source station enables a new byte onto the data bus, the SH function enters (C) and waits.

5. The function re-enters (A) if the status of the station changes and it is no longer either an active talker, controller, or responder to a serial poll.

6. Once the source station senses that all acceptors are ready for more data (i.e. all acceptors have de-asserted the NRFD line), the SH function enters (D).

7. Once the source station senses that all acceptors have accepted the data (i.e. all acceptors have de-asserted the NDAC line), the SH function enters (E) and waits for a new data transfer cycle to start.

8. The function enters (F) if the status of the station changes and it is no longer either an active talker, controller, or responder to a serial poll.

9. If the station instrumentation causes the data byte to be removed from the bus, the SH function re-enters (B) to wait for its return.

10. The function enters (F) if the status of the station changes and it is no longer either an active talker, controller, or responder to a serial poll.

11. If the station status changes, returning it to a role of active talker, controller, or serial poll responder; the function will exit (F) and enter (E) to resume waiting for a new data cycle to begin.

12. If the station instrumentation causes the data byte to be removed from the bus, the SH function will exit (F) and enter (A).

to force the addressed station to accept remote commands from the controller instead of just local commands from the station device's own front panel. A station can request service from the controller by asserting the *service request* (SRQ) line. The SRQ drivers of all the stations are wire-ORed on the bus, and the controller will only sense that SRQ has been asserted. In order to identify which device is requesting service, the controller will have to conduct either a parallel or serial poll.

INTERFACE FUNCTIONS

The IEEE 488 standard specifies network operation in terms of *functions* that are executed by the various stations in the system. Each of these functions is in turn completely specified by a set of states and a set of rules governing transitions between these states. A simplified discussion of several of these functions will be presented, but the complete specifications needed to actually design an IEEE 488 device should be obtained directly from the standard itself.

Device Trigger Function. The device trigger (DT) function allows a station to begin normal operation. This function will generally be used after the station has been initialized and set up as required by the controller. Details of the DT function are illustrated in the state diagram of Fig. 15-2.

Source Handshake Function. A station transmitting a data byte uses the source handshake (SH) function to insure proper transfer of the byte. The operation of the SH function executing in the source station must interlock with the operation of the acceptor handshake functions operating in all the destination stations. Details of the SH function are illustrated in the state diagram of Fig. 15-3.

Acceptor Handshake Function. A station that is receiving a data byte uses the acceptor handshake (AH) function to insure proper reception of the byte. The operation of the AH function executing in a destination station must interlock with the operation of the SH function executing in the source device. Details of the AH function are illustrated in the state diagram of Fig. 15-4.

Talker Function. A station that has been addressed to talk by the controller, uses the talker (T) function to transmit station dependent data or station status data over the data bus to other stations. Status data is transmitted in response to a serial poll issued by the controller. The T function is actually two subfunctions—one is concerned with normal talker operation and the other is concerned with the enabling response to a serial poll. Details of both subfunctions are illustrated in the state diagram of Fig. 15-5.

Listener Function. A station that has been addressed to listen by the controller uses the listener (L) function, to receive station dependent data via the data bus from other stations. Details of the L function are illustrated in the state diagram of Fig. 15-6.

Service Request Function. Any station in need of service by the controller can use the service request (SR) function to alert the controller to this need. The SRQ line of the general interface management bus is asserted by the SR function and acts as an interrupt to the controller. Details of the SR function are illustrated in the state diagram of Fig. 15-7.

Remote Local Function. The remote local (RL) function allows a station to select whether it will accept input information from a remote source via the bus or from its local front panel controls. Details of the RL function are illustrated in the state diagram of Fig. 15-8.

Device Clear Function. The device clear (DC) function allows a station to

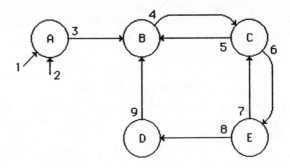

(A) - **acceptor idle state (AIDS)**--The AH function is inactive, and the NRFD and NDAC lines are not asserted.

(B) - **acceptor not ready state (ANRS)**--The AH function is preparing to continue with the handshake cycle. The NRFD and NDAC lines are asserted.

(C) - **acceptor ready state (ACRS)**--The AH function is ready to receive data and indicates this by de-asserting the NRFD line.

(D) - **acceptor wait for new cycle state (AWNS)**--The AH function has received a data byte and indicates this by asserting NRFD and de-asserting NDAC.

(E) - **accept data state (ACDS)**--The AH function accepts a byte from the data bus and, if the station's L function is in the listener active state, makes it available to the local instrumentation. The NRFD and NDAC lines are asserted.

Fig. 15-4. State diagram of the GPIB acceptor handshake (AH) function.

1. The AH function powers up in (A).

2. The AH function will exit any state and return to (A) if the controller is not sending a command and the station is not an active listener.

3. Whenever the acceptor becomes an active listener or senses that the ATN line has been asserted (indicating that the controller is sending an interface command) its AH function will enter (B).

4. When the acceptor becomes ready to accept a data byte it will enter (C).

5. The AH function will return to (B) if the acceptor is an active listener and the local instrumentation indicates that it is not ready for data.

6. Upon sensing that the source station has asserted the DAV line, the AH function will enter (E).

7. If the controller seizes control of the network in the middle of a talker-listener handshake exchange, the acceptor (listener) may be accepting data in state (E) when the controller forces the talker to prematurely de-assert the DAV line. If the acceptor senses de-assertion of DAV, the AH function will return to (C).

8. If while in (E) the acceptor senses that ATN has been asserted by the controller, the AH function will enter (D).

9. Once the acceptor senses that the source has de-asserted DAV, the AH function will return to (A).

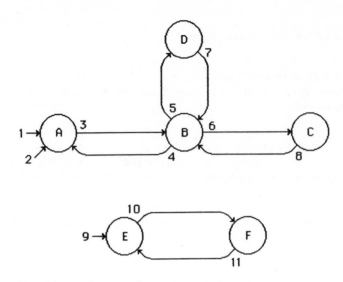

(A) - **talker idle state (TIDS)**--The T function is not active and the data bus outputs are allowed to float.

(B) - **talker addressed state (TADS)**-- The station has been addressed to talk and is preparing to do so.

(C) - **talker active state (TACS)**--The local instrumentation places a data byte onto the data bus under the control of the SH function.

(D) - **serial poll active state (SPAS)**--The T function enables the local instrumentation to place its status byte onto the data bus.

(E) - **serial poll idle state (SPIS)**--The station is not enabled to respond to a serial poll.

(F) - **serial poll mode state (SPMS)**--The station is enabled to respond if a serial poll should be received.

Fig. 15-5. State diagram of the GPIB talker (T) function.

Note: States (E) and (F) exist in parallel with the other states. The T function can be in either (E) or (F) and simultaneously be in one of the other states as well.

1. The T function powers up in (A).

2. The T function will exit any state and return to (A) if the system controller issues an interface clear (IFC) command.

3. Once the station is addressed to talk, its T function will enter (B).

4. If the station was addressed as part of a talk address group and detects the address of another station while waiting to send data, the T function will return to (A).

5. If the station is responding to a serial poll, the T function will pass immediately through (B) and enter (D).

6. If the ATN line is not asserted and the station is not responding to a serial poll, the T function will pass immediately through (B) and enter (C).

7. If the controller elects to issue a command it will assert the ATN line. If the talker senses ATN true while responding to a serial poll, its T function will return to (B) relinquishing the bus to the controller.

8. If the talker senses ATN true while outputing data, its T function will return to (B) relinquishing the bus to the controller.

9. The serial poll response capability powers up in (E).

10. If the station receives a serial poll enable message, the serial poll response capability will enter (F).

11. The serial poll response capability will return to (E) if the station receives either an interface clear command or a serial poll disable message.

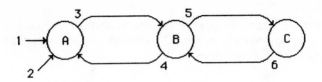

(A) - **listener idle state (LIDS)**--The L function is not active.

(B) - **listener addressed state (LADS)**--The station has been addressed to listen and is preparing to do so.

(C) - **listener active state (LACS)**--The station accepts a byte from the data bus under control of the AH function and makes the byte available to the local instrumentation.

1. The L function powers up in (A).

2. The L function will exit any state and return to (A) if the system controller issues an interface clear command.

3. Once the listener is addressed, its L function will enter (B).

4. The L function will return to (A) if the station receives an unlisten command from the controller.

5. If the ATN line is not asserted, the L function will pass immediately through (B) and enter (C).

6. If the controller elects to issue a command, it will assert the ATN line. When the listener senses ATN true, its L function will return to (B).

Fig. 15-6. State diagram of the GPIB listener (L) function.

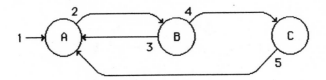

(A) - **negative poll response state (NPRS)**--The station's SR function is not requesting service, and therefore the SRQ output is not asserted.

(B) - **service request state (SRQS)**--The SR function indicates that the station requires service from the controller by asserting the output to the SRQ line.

(C) - **affirmative poll response state (APRS)**--The station requires service from the controller, and the SR function causes the T function to include a request for service in the serial poll response being concurrent with this state.

1. The SR function powers up in (A).

2. Whenever the station instrumentation requires service from the controller and the station is not responding to a serial poll, the SR function will enter (B).

3. The SR function will exit (B) and return to the idle state (A) if the instrumentation's request for service is cancelled.

4. When the stations are polled by the controller to determine the source of the service request, the requesting station's SR function will enter (C) and issue an RQS response under control of the T function.

5. The SR function will exit (C) and return to the idle state (A) if the instrumentation's request for service is cancelled.

Fig. 15-7. State diagram of the GPIB service request (SR) function.

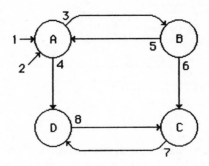

(A) - **local state (LOCS)**--In this state the station
instrumentation accepts control inputs only from the local front
panel.

(B) - **remote state (REMS)**--In this state the station
instrumentation accepts control inputs from the network rather
than from the local front panel. (However the station can still
accept a **return to local** command from the local
instrumentation.

(C) - **remote with lockout state (RWLS)**--In this state the
station instrumentation accepts control inputs from the network
instead of from the local front panel. Operation in (C) is similar
to operation in (B) except the station will not accept a **return to
local** request from the local instrumentation while in (C).

Fig. 15-8. State diagram of the GPIB remote/local (RL) function.

(D) - **local with lockout state (LWLS)**--In this state the station instrumentation accepts control inputs only from the local front panel. Operation in this state is identical to operation in (A) with only one difference. In (A) an active **return to local** request from the local instrumentation prevents entry into remote operation, but in (D) the RL function ignores any **return to local** request which may be issued.

1. The RL function powers up in (A).

2. The RL function will return to (A) if at any time the REN line is de-asserted by the controller.

3. If REN is asserted, the station is addressed, and the station instrumentation is not issuing a **return to local** request, the RL function will enter (B).

4. If REN is asserted and the station receives a **local lockout** command from the controller, the station's RL function will enter state (D).

5. The RL function will exit (B) and return to (A) on command from either the system controller or the local station instrumentation.

6. If the station receives a **local lockout** command from the controller, the station's RL function will exit (B) and enter (C).

7. On command from the system controller, the RL function will exit (C) and enter (D).

8. If the station is addressed while in (D), its RL function will enter (C).

initialize itself when so directed by the controller. Details of this function are illustrated in the state diagram of Fig. 15-9.

Parallel Poll Function. The parallel poll (PP) function provides a station with the capability to respond to a parallel poll issued by the controller. Up to eight stations can respond at the same time with each station assigned one bit of the data bus. Details of this function are illustrated in Fig. 15-10.

Control Function. One or more stations in each GPIB network will have the capability to control the operation of the network. These capabilities are provided by the control (C) function which is illustrated in Fig. 15-11. One of these controllers must possess additional system controller capabilities which are illustrated in Fig. 15-12.

ELECTRICAL CHARACTERISTICS

The electrical specifications for the GPIB are based on the use of TTL circuits as drivers and receivers. Open collector drivers must be used to drive the SRQ, NRFD, and NDAC signal lines since these lines must support a distributed "wired-OR" function.

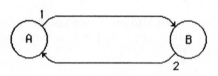

(A)- **device clear idle state (DCIS)**--The DC function is not active.

(B)- **device clear active state (DCAS)**--The DC function issues a clear signal to the local instrumentation. The instrumentation can use this signal to reset itself to some predefined status.

1. Upon command from the controller, a station's DC function will exit (A) and enter (B).

2. When the command from the controller is de-asserted, the DC function will return to (A).

Fig. 15-9. State diagram of the GPIB device clear (DC) function.

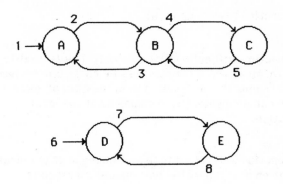

(A)- **parallel poll idle state (PPIS)**--The PP function is
inactive and the station is not able to respond to a parallel poll.

(B)- **parallel poll standby state (PPSS)**--The PP function is
enabled to respond to parallel polls if they should occur.

(C)- **parallel poll active state (PPAS)**--The PP function is
responding to a parallel poll, and will assert the particular data
bus line assigned by the **parallel poll enable** message
previously received from the controller.

(D)- **parallel poll unaddressed to configure state (PUCS)**
The PP function is set to ignore any **parallel poll enable** or
parallel poll disable messages which may be issued by the
controller.

(E)- **parallel poll addressed to configure state (PACS)**
The PP function is set to accept any **parallel poll enable** or
parallel poll disable messages which may be issued by the
controller.

Fig. 15-10. State diagram of the GPIB parallel poll (PP) function.

1. The PP function powers up in Ⓐ.

2. The PP function will enter Ⓑ if a **parallel poll enable** message is received while the station's PP configuration-enable feature is in Ⓔ and the AH function is in the **accept data state**. The function can also enter Ⓑ on command of the local instrumentation.

3. The PP function will return to Ⓐ on command of the local instrumentation or if a parallel poll disable message is received while the station's PP configuration-enable feature is in Ⓔ and the AH function is in the **accept data state**. The function can also enter Ⓔ if a **parallel poll unconfigure** message is received while the AH function is in the **accept data state**.

4. The PP function will enter Ⓒ within 200 nanoseconds of sensing that both the EOI and ATN lines are asserted.

5. The PP function will return to Ⓑ within 200 nanoseconds of sensing that either EOI or ATN has been de-asserted.

6. The configuration enable feature of the PP function powers up in Ⓓ.

7. The configuration enable feature will enter Ⓔ if a **parallel poll configure** message is received while the L function is in the **listener addressed state** and the AH function is in the **accept data state**.

8. The configuration enable feature will return to Ⓓ upon acceptance of a **primary command group** message from the controller.

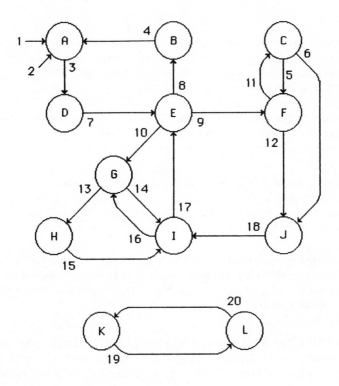

(A) - **controller idle state (CIDS)** -- The controller capabilities of the station are not enabled.

(B) - **controller transfer state (CTRS)** -- The station is sending a take control command to another station, directing it to become the new controller-in-charge. The ATN line is asserted

(C) - **controller standby hold state (CSHS)** -- The station has been directed by its local instrumentation to synchronously take control of the network, but it is waiting for at least 1.5 μsec before proceeding.

(D) - **controller addressed state (CADS)** -- The station has been addressed by the controller-in-charge and instructed to become the new controller-in-charge, but it is waiting for the old controller-in-charge to de-assert the ATN line.

Fig. 15-11. State diagram of the GPIB control (C) function. (Continued through page 194.)

(E) - **controller active state (CACS)**--The C function accepts a command byte from the local instrumentation and outputs it to the data bus under control of the SH function. The ATN line is asserted during this state.

(F) - **controller standby state (CSBS)**--The station is still the controller-in-charge, but it has relinquished use of the data bus to a talker station elsewhere in the network.

(G) - **controller parallel poll wait state (CPWS)**--The C function is issuing a parallel poll request and is waiting for the response on the data bus to become valid. Both the ATN and EOI lines are asserted.

(H) - **controller parallel poll state (CPPS)**--The C function accepts the poll response byte from the data bus and makes it available to the controller instrumentation. Both the ATN and EOI lines are de-asserted.

(I) - **controller active wait state (CAWS)**--The parallel poll has ended, but the C function is waiting for at least 1.5 μsec to insure that all stations have stopped responding before it returns to E .

(J) - **controller synchronous wait state (CSWS)**--The C function has been ordered by the controller station's local instrumentation to take control of the network and therefore asserts the ATN line. The C function waits in this state for at least 500 nanoseconds to insure that any active talker on the network senses the assertion of ATN and consequently relinquishes the bus as required.

(K) - **controller service not requested state (CSNS)**--The C function indicates to the controller's local instrumentation that one or more stations on the network are requesting service from the controller.

1. The C function powers up in (A).

2. The C function will exit any state and return to (A) if the station is not the system controller and another station which is the system controller asserts the IFC line.

3. Upon accepting a **take control** message from the controller-in-charge, the C function will enter (D) .

4. When the station's SH function indicates that a **take control** message has been sent to and accepted by another station, the C function will return to (A) .

5. The C function will exit (C) and return to (F) if the local instrumentation cancels its request for the station to synchronously take control of the network.

6. The C function will enter (J) after waiting in (C) for at least 1.5 microseconds.

7. Upon sensing that the old controller-in-charge has de-asserted ATN, the C function will exit (D) and assume the role of controller-in-charge by entering (E) .

8. After issuing a **take control** command to another station, the C function will enter (B) .

9. The C function will exit (E) and enter (F) when ordered by the local instrumentation, provided that the SH function is not in either the **source transfer state** or the **source delay state**.

10. The C function will exit (E) and enter (G) when the local instrumentation orders a parallel poll to be conducted, provided that the SH function is not in either the **source transfer state** or the **source delay state**.

11. The C function will exit (F) and enter (C) when the local instrumentation has issued a request for the station to synchronously take control of the network and the station's AH function is in the **acceptor not ready state**.

12. The C function will exit (F) and enter (J) when the local instrumentation requests it to asynchronously take control of the network.

13. After waiting at least 2 microseconds, the C function will exit (G) and enter (H).

14. The C function will exit (G) and enter (I) if the local instrumentation cancels its request for the station to conduct a parallel poll.

15. The C function will exit (H) and enter (I) if the local instrumentation cancels its request for the station to conduct a parallel poll.

16. The C function will enter (G) if the local instrumentation issues a request for the station to conduct a parallel poll.

17. After waiting in state (I) for at least 1.5 microseconds, the C function will enter (E) if the local instrumentation is not requesting a parallel poll.

18. The C function will exit (J) and enter (I) if the T function is in the **talker addressed state** or if at least 500 nanoseconds has elapsed since entering (J).

19. The C function will enter (L) upon sensing that another station is requesting service from the controller (i.e. the SRQ line is asserted).

20. The C function will enter (K) upon sensing that no station is requesting service from the controller (i.e. the SRQ line is de-asserted).

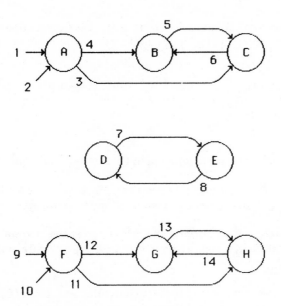

(A) - **system control remote enable idle state (SRIS)**
The controller is not the system controller and is incapable of asserting the REN line.

(B) - **system control remote enable active state (SRAS)**
The system controller is enabling remote operation of other stations. The REN line is asserted.

(C) - **system control remote enable not active state (SRNS)**
The controller is the system controller, but it is not currently asserting the REN line.

(D) - **system control not active state (SNAS)** -- The C function is prohibited from exercising its system controller features.

(E) - **system control active state (SACS)** -- The controller is enabled to exercise its system controller features.

Fig. 15-12. State diagram of system control features of the GPIB control function.

$\widehat{F}$ - **system control interface clear idle state (SIIS)** -- The controller is not the system controller and is incapable of asserting the IFC line.

$\widehat{G}$ - **system control interface clear active state (SIAS)** The system controller is clearing the interface. The IFC line is asserted.

$\widehat{H}$ - **system control interface clear not active state (SINS)** The controller is the system controller, but it is not currently asserting the IFC line.

1. The C function's remote enable capability powers up in $\widehat{A}$.

2. The C function's remote enable capability will exit any state and return to $\widehat{A}$ if the controller loses its system controller role.

3. The C function will enter $\widehat{C}$ if the controller is the system controller and its instrumentation is not ordering a remote enable signal to be sent.

4. The C function of an active system controller will enter $\widehat{B}$ if it has been in state $\widehat{A}$ for at least 100 µsec and the instrumentation orders a remote enable signal to be sent.

5. The C function will enter $\widehat{C}$ if the instrumentation stops ordering that a remote enable signal be sent.

6. The C function will enter $\widehat{B}$ if the instrumentation orders that a remote enable signal be sent.

7. The C function will enter $\widehat{E}$ when so ordered by the local instrumentation.

8. The C function will enter $\widehat{D}$ when so ordered by the local instrumentation.

9. The C function's interface clearing capability powers up in $\widehat{F}$.

10. The C function's interface clearing capability will exit any state and return to $\widehat{F}$ if the controller loses its system controller role.

11. The C function will enter $\widehat{H}$ if the controller is the system controller and its instrumentation is not ordering an interface clear signal to be sent.

12. The C function of an active system controller will enter state Ⓖ if it has been in state Ⓐ for at least 100 µsec and the instrumentation orders an interface clear signal to be sent.

13. The C function will enter Ⓗ after the instrumentation has stopped ordering an interface clear signal for at least 100 µsec.

14. The C function will enter Ⓖ if the instrumentation orders that an interface clear signal be sent.

Chapter 16

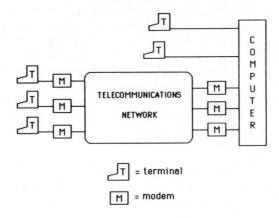

$\boxed{\text{⌐T}}$ = terminal

$\boxed{\text{M}}$ = modem

LAN Options

M OST OF THE MATERIALS PRESENTED IN THIS BOOK HAS BEEN GENERAL PUR-
pose theory and techniques that are applicable in a variety of datacomm situations. In Chapters 14 and 15 we examined two of the most predominant networking
standards—Ethernet and IEEE 488. In this chapter we will survey some specific prod-
uct implementations, which, while not as pervasive as Ethernet or IEEE 488, are
still important alternatives. These products include hardware and software that are
available for use in general RS-232 and RS-449/422/423 environments as well as the
specific I/O environments of the IBM PC, Apple II family, and Apple Macintosh.
This chapter is not intended to be a buyer's guide or even an exhaustive, all-inclusive
enumeration of brandname products—in today's market conditions such an effort would
rapidly become outdated. Instead, the emphasis will be on presenting a representative sampling of the <u>kinds</u> of things that are available.

RECENT TRENDS

In the early days of LAN development a great debate raged on as to which standards were the best standards—particularly in the area of data-link control standards.
Recently much of this debate has subsided; emerging in its place is a consensus that
no one particular data-link standard is best, but different datalinks are best for different applications. Ethernet and its derivatives seem to predominate in the office
environment, and IEEE 488 is the unchallenged leader in the laboratory environment. A number of other approaches, led perhaps by token-bus schemes, are preferred in industrial environments. Of course IBM is still IBM and their announcement
of a token passing ring scheme for 1986 still has many vendors and customers alike
waiting and guessing.

NETWORKING FOR THE IBM PC

Despite the hopes of Apple chairman Steve Jobs and other would-be giant killers, the IBM PC and its descendants will be the major de facto standard in personal-sized business computers for the foreseeable future. Therefore, any serious general-purpose networking scheme must be designed to work within the limitations and idiosyncracies of the PC. As might be expected, a number of suppliers eyed the huge and growing installed base of PCs and decided to offer networking products designed specifically for the PC. Some of these products use established standards like Ethernet, and others use specially developed proprietary networking schemes. Each approach has advantages and disadvantages and selecting the best one will depend heavily on the requirements of a specific application.

The IBM PC is an *open system,* which means that the internal bus of the machine has expansion slots on it that allow the owner to interface peripheral devices directly to the system bus. Thus for data communications the user has a choice—stand alone modems or network interface units equipped with RS-232 or similar serial interfaces can be connected by simply installing the appropriate serial interface card in one of the bus slots. On the other hand, a large variety of modem and network interface designs are now available on printed circuit cards which plug directly into a slot on the bus, completely eliminating the need for a serial interface. A number of PC networking products are summarized in Figs. 16-1 through 16-7. In addition, Ethernet products from 3Com, Interlan, and Ungermann-Bass support networks of PCs as well as a number of other small computers. As if all these third-party offerings weren't enough, IBM has recently unveiled PC Network, which is a broadband CSMA/CD network which operates at 2 Mbps and supports up to 72 users. The PC Network software and the DOS 3.1 operating system required to support it are scheduled for release in early 1985. If the software is good, PC Network could become a serious threat to all of the third-party network suppliers.

THE APPLE II FAMILY

Like the PC, members of the Apple II family are open systems with expansion slots which will accommodate either general-purpose serial interfaces or dedicated modem and networking circuit boards. Although the Apple II has been around somewhat longer than the PC, the variety of dedicated networking products is not as great. This can be attributed to the fact that large offices are the primary LAN users and large offices tend to buy PCs rather than Apples. Note however, that Omninet (which is summarized in Fig. 16-5) supports the Apple II family as well as the IBM PC. Many other networks can also be used via a serial interface such as RS-232.

APPLE MACINTOSH

The Macintosh is a *closed system* that has no internal expansion slots that interface to the system bus. Therefore, all add-ons to the basic system must be connected through I/O ports. There are dedicated I/O ports for the mouse, keyboard, printer, and add-on disk drive. There is also an RS-422-A compatible port intended for a modem, but which can be used for a variety of serially-interfaced devices. This port will operate at speeds up a 230.4 Kbps when clocked by the computer and at speeds up to 920 Kbps when clocked by an external source connected to pin 7 of the interface connector. As discussed in Chapter 8, RS-422-A defines only the electrical characteristics and is intended to be used with RS-449, which defines circuit functions and physical characteristics. The serial ports on the Macintosh use pin assignments, shown in Fig.

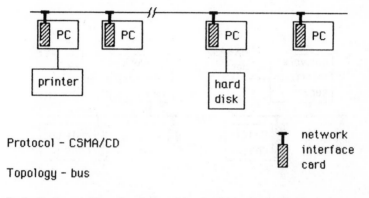

PCnet

Orchid Technology, Inc.
17790 Westinghouse Drive
Fremont, CA   94539

(415) 490-8586

Protocol – CSMA/CD

Topology – bus

Data Rate – 1 Mbps is claimed by Orchid. An independent
reviewer indicates that 880 kbps is more accurate.

Medium – RG 59B/U coaxial cable (3000 feet maximum) or
RG 11/U coaxial cable (7000 feet maximum)

Computers supported – IBM PC (DOS 1.1 or DOS 2.0 but not both
in the same network)

Remarks – A PC-XT can be used as a hard disk server and still
be used locally. This network will also allow shared
use of a printer attached to one of the PC s, but true
print server or spooler capabilities needed in
print-intensive installations are not yet available.

Fig. 16-1. Features of PCnet by Orchid Technology.

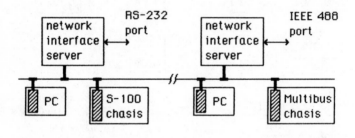

DESNET

The Destek Group
830 C East Evelyn Ave
Sunnyvale, CA 94086

(408) 737-7211

Protocol - CSMA/CD

Topology - bus

Data Rate - 2 Mbps

Medium - RG 59/U coaxial cable (2000 feet maximum)

Computers supported - IBM PC (PC DOS, MS-DOS, CP/M, UNIX)
S-100 and Multibus sytems
RS-232, RS-422, & IEEE 488

Fig. 16-2. Features of DESNET by The Destek Group.

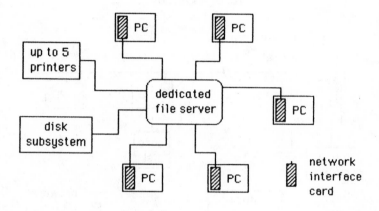

NetWare S

Novell, Inc.
1170 North Industrial Park Drive
Orem, UT 84057

(800) 453-1267

Protocol – proprietary

Topology – star (24 PCs maximum)

Data Rate – 500 kbps

Medium – shielded twisted pair (1000 meter maximum)

Computers supported – IBM PC (PC DOS V1.1, V1.2, V2.0;
                              CP/M; CP/M-86)

Remarks – Network supports five serial printer ports from
          50 to 19.2K baud. There is a 68000-based dedicated
          file server located at the hub of the star.

Fig. 16-3. Features of NetWare S by Novell, Inc.

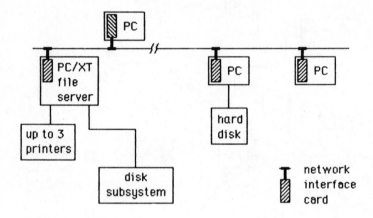

NetWare X

Novell, Inc.
1170 North Industrial Park Drive
Orem, UT 84057

(800) 453-1267

Protocol – proprietary

Topology – bus

Data Rate – 1.43 Mbps

Medium – RG-59/U (1300 meters maximum)

Computers supported – IBM PC (PC DOS V1.1, V1.2, V2.0;
CP/M; CP/M-86)

Remarks – Network supports one parallel and two serial
printer ports. The file server is an IBM PC/XT.

Fig. 16-4. Features of NetWare X by Novell, Inc.

```
┌─────────────────────────────────────────────────────────────┐
│                                                               │
│                    ┌──────────────┐                           │
│                    │   Omninet    │                           │
│                    └──────────────┘                           │
│                                                               │
│                    Corvus Systems, Inc.                       │
│                    2029 O'Toole Avenue                        │
│                    San Jose, CA 95131                         │
│                    (408) 946-7700                             │
│                                                               │
│     Protocol - proprietary CSMA                               │
│                                                               │
│     Topology - bus                                            │
│                                                               │
│     Data Rate - 1 Mbps                                        │
│                                                               │
│     Medium - twisted pair (4000 feet maximum)                 │
│                                                               │
│     Computers supported - IBM PC; Corvus Concept; Apple II,   │
│                           IIe, III; DEC Rainbow; TI           │
│                           Professional; Zenith Z100           │
│                                                               │
│     Remarks - The network supports sharing of Corvus          │
│               Winchester disk units. Print servers, and SNA   │
│               gateway servers are available now, with         │
│               Ethernet, broadband, and X.25 gateways planned  │
│               for the future.                                 │
│                                                               │
└─────────────────────────────────────────────────────────────┘
```

Fig. 16-5. Features of Omninet by Corvus Systems.

16-8, that do not comply with RS-449. As mentioned in Chapter 8, RS-423-A can be made to interoperate with RS-232-C, but in general, RS-422-A drivers will not interoperate with RS-232-C receivers. In spite of both this fact and the fact that most Macintosh literature classifies the serial ports as "RS-422," devices employing RS-232-C, RS-423-A, and RS-422-A can all be successfully interfaced to these ports. This is so because the serial port outputs are driven by AM26LS30C driver ICs that are equipped with a mode control that permits them to be configured as either two RS-422-A balanced drivers or four RS-423-A unbalanced drivers. The Macintosh is a relatively new machine and the third-party supplier system has not been operating for very long, but one Macintosh-specific network is summarized in Fig. 16-9.

IEEE 802

The IEEE 802 committee set out to establish a local area networking standard that would bring some order to the chaotic flood of different proprietary standards being developed. After some initial study of the problem, the committee realized that one

```
┌─────────────────────────────────────────────┐
│                 ┌───────────┐                │
│                 │ Multi Link│                │
│                 └───────────┘                │
│                                              │
│              Davong Systems, Inc.            │
│              217 Humboldt Court              │
│              Sunnyvale, CA 94086             │
│                                              │
│              (408) 734-4900                  │
│                                              │
│       Protocol - IEEE 802.4 token passing    │
│                                              │
│       Topology - arbitrary                   │
│                                              │
│       Data Rate - 2.5 Mbps                   │
│                                              │
│       Medium - RG-62/U coaxial cable         │
│                                              │
│       Computers supported - IBM PC           │
└─────────────────────────────────────────────┘
```

Fig. 16-6. Features of Multi Link by Davong Systems.

```
┌─────────────────────────────────────────────┐
│                 ┌─────────┐                  │
│                 │  G/NET  │                  │
│                 └─────────┘                  │
│                                              │
│            Gateway Communications            │
│            16782 Redhill Avenue              │
│            Irvine, CA  92714                 │
│                                              │
│            (714) 261-0762                    │
│                                              │
│   Protocol - CSMA-CA/CD                      │
│                                              │
│   Topology - bus                             │
│                                              │
│   Data Rate - 1.43 Mbps                      │
│                                              │
│   Medium - RG-59/U (4000 feet maximum)       │
│            RG-11/U (7000 feet maximum)       │
│                                              │
│   Computers supported - IBM PC (DOS 1.1, DOS 2.0, CP/M-86) │
│                                              │
│   Remarks - X.25 and SNA gateways are available │
└─────────────────────────────────────────────┘
```

Fig. 16-7. Features of G/NET by Gateway Communications.

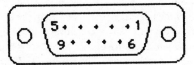

1. Ground
2. +5 volts
3. Ground
4. transmit data +
5. transmit data -
6. +12 volts
7. external clock
   or carrier detect
8. receive data +
9. receive data -

female connector
on Macintosh

Fig. 16-8. Pin assignments for Macintosh serial interface ports.

MacLink

Davong Systems, Inc.
217 Humboldt Court
Sunnyvale, CA 94086

(408) 734-4900

Protocol - SDLC   Data Rate - 1 Mbps

Topology - Loop   Maximum Nodes - 64

Medium - coaxial cable

Computers supported - Apple Macintosh

Fig. 16-9. Features of MacLink from Davong Systems.

single standard could not possibly encompass the various speed, distance, sizing, reliability, cabling, and operational requirements imposed by a multitude of different potential LAN applications. Therefore the 802 standardization efforts were split into several different areas. A CSMA/CD system similar to Ethernet is defined in IEEE 802.3, while 802.4 and 802.5 define token-passing bus and token-passing ring networks, respectively. Representatives from various manufacturers sit on the committees which are working on the standards. Naturally, each manufacturer would like to set standards that are compatible with their own existing products, and in the high-stakes arena of LAN standards this has led to a great deal of controversy and argument between opposing factions. In order to get anything at all approved by most members of the committee some compromises must be made, and the resulting standard may or may not be as technically sound as some similar proprietary standards. For this reason many of the products available in the immediate future will likely adhere to de facto standards which are determined instead by marketplace reaction to the offerings of major manufacturers.

Acronyms
and Abbreviations

AC—alternating current
ACDS—accept data state
ACK—acknowledge
ACAS—acceptor ready state
AH—acceptor handshake
AIDS—acceptor idle state
AM—amplitude modulation
AMI—alternate mark inversion
ANRS—acceptor not ready state
ANSI—American National Standards Institute
APRS—affirmative poll response state
ASCII—American Standard Code for Information Interchange
ASK—amplitude-shift keying
ATN—attention
AWG—American wire gage
AWNS—acceptor wait for new cycle state
BCC—block check character
BCD—binary coded decimal
BER—bit error rate
BOP—bit-oriented protocol
BPS—bits per second
BS—backspace
C—controller *or* control
CACS—controller active state

CADS—controller addressed state

CAN—cancel

CATV—community antenna television (originally) *or* cable television (through common usage)

CAWS—controller active wait state

CCITT—Comite' Consultatif Internationale de Télégraphique et Telephonique (often Anglicized as Consultative Committee in International Telegraphy and Telephony)

CIDS—controller idle state

CMOS—complemetary metal oxide semiconductor

CPPS—controller parallel poll state

CPWS—controller parallel poll wait state

CR—carriage return

CRC—cyclic redundancy check(ing)

CSBS—controller standby state

CSHS—controller standby hold state

CSMA—carrier-sense multiple access

CSMA/CA—carrier-sense multiple access with collision avoidance

CSMA/CD—carrier-sense multiple access with collision detection

CSNS—controller service not requested state

CSWS—controller synchronous wait state

CTRS—controller transfer state

CTS-clear to send

DAA—data access arrangement *or* data access adaptor

DAV—data valid

dB—decibel

dc—device clear *or* direct current

DCAS—device clear active state

DCE—data circuit-terminating equipment *or* data communications equipment

DCIS—device clear idle state

DES—Data Encryption Standard

DIO—data input/output

DLE—data-link escape

DPSK—differential phase-shift keying

DSB—double sideband

DSR—data set ready

DT—device trigger

DTAC—device trigger active state

DTE—data terminal equipment

DTIS—device trigger idle state

DTMF—dual tone multifrequency

DTR—data terminal ready

DUX—duplex

ETX—end of text

EM—end of medium

EIA—Electronic Industries Association

EDAC—error detection and correction

EBCDIC—extended binary-coded decimal interchange code
ENQ—enquiry
EOI—end or identify
EOT—end of text
ETB—end of transmission block
ESC—escape
EMC—electromagnetic compatibility
EMI—electromagnetic interference
FCC—Federal Communications Commission
FDM—frequency division multiplexing
FF—form feed
FM—frequency modulation
FS—file separator
FSK—frequency-shift keying
GPIB—General Purpose Interface Bus
GS—group separator
HDLC—high-level data-link control
HT—horizontal tab
IEEE—Institute of Electrical and Electronics Engineers
IFC—interface clear
ISO—International Organization for Standardization
ITU—International Telecommunications Union
L—listener
LACS—listener active state
LADS—listener addressed state
LAN—local area network
LF—line feed
LIDS—listener idle state
LOCS—local state
LRC—longitudunal redundancy check
LSI—large scale integration
LWLS—local with lockout state
MSI—medium scale integration
MUX—multiplexer
NAK—negative acknowledge
NDAC—not data accepted
NPRS—negative poll response state
NRFD—not ready for data
NRZ—nonreturn to zero
NRZI—nonreturn to zero inverted
OCS—office communications system
OOK—on-off keying
PACS—parallel poll addressed to configure state
PLL—phase-locked loop
PM—phase modulation
PP—parallel poll
PPAS—parallel poll active state
PPIS—parallel poll idle state
PPSS—parallel poll standby state
PSK—phase-shift keying
PUCS—parallel poll unaddressed to configure state

QAM—quadrature amplitude modulation
REMS—remote state
REN—remote enable
rf—radio frequency
RFI—radio frequency interference
RI—ring indicator
RIU—ring interface unit
RJE—remote job entry
RL—remote/local
RS—record separator
RTL—return to local
RTS—request to send
RWLS—remote with lockout state
RX—receive
SACS—system control active state
SDLC—synchronous data link control
SDYS—source delay state
SGNS—source generate state
SH—source handshake
SI—shift in
SIAS—system control interface clear active state
SIDS—source idle state
SIIS—system control interface clear idle state
SINS—system control interface clear not active state
SIWS—source idle wait state
SNAS—system control not active state
SO—shift out
SOH—start of heading
SPAS—serial poll active state
SPIS—serial poll idle state
SPMS—serial poll mode state
SR—service request
SRAS—system control remote enable active state
SRIS—system control remote enable idle state
SRNS—system control remote enable not active state
SRQ—service request
SRQS—service request state
SSB—single sideband
SSI—small scale integration
STRS—source transfer state
STX—start of text
SUB—substitute
SWNS—source wait for new cycle state
SYN—synchronous idle
T—talker
TACS—talker active state
TADS—talker addressed state
TDM—time division multiplexing
TIDS—talker idle state
TTL—transistor-transistor logic
TTY—teletype

Tx—transmit
US—unit separator
UART—universal asynchronous receiver/transmitter
USART—universal synchronous/asynchronouos
  receiver/transmitter
USRT—universal synchronous receiver/transmitter
VRC—vertical redundancy check
VSB—vestigial sideband
VT—vertical tab

Glossary

acknowledgement—A response sent to indicate receipt of a particular message or portion (block) of a message.

ALOHA network—A radio-linked local area network developed at the University of Hawaii.

alternate mark inversion coding—A bipolar line coding scheme in which spaces are encoded as zero signal levels and marks are encoded as nonzero levels which alternate between positive and negative for successive marks. (See Fig. 4-11.)

American National Standards Institute—An organization concerned with standardization in many areas of commerce and technology, including electronics, data processing, and communications. Information concerning ANSI publications may be obtained from:
American National Standards Institute
1430 Broadway
New York, NY 10018

American Standard Code for Information Interchange—A standard seven-bit data code adopted by ANSI and which enjoys worldwide usage. (See Table 2-9.)

American Wire Gage—A standardized system for specification of wire sizes.

amplitude modulation—A modulation scheme in which the amplitude of a constant-frequency sinusoidal carrier is varied as a function of the baseband signal. (See Fig. 6-1.)

amplitude-shift keying—A form of amplitude modulation in which the amplitude of the carrier can assume only a few discrete levels.

angle modulation—A general category of modulation techniques which includes both phase modulation and frequency modulation.

applications layer—The portion of the ISO OSI model which is concerned with the interface between the applications software and the presentation layer.

asynchronous data transmission—An operating mode in which there is no intentional bit synchronization between the transmitting and receiving devices. In start-stop operation, which is the most prevalent form of asynchronous transmission, start and stop bits are used to indicate the beginning and end of each character.

asynchronous TDM—A time division multiplexing scheme in which the data transfers from the individual to the multiplexers make use of an asynchronous start-stop format. This complicates multiplexer design since a number of different user data streams of different and arbitrarily related data rates must be combined into a single, constant-rate composite data stream.

attenuation—A reduction in the strength or power of a signal.

balanced transmission—A method for transmission of baseband data in which each signal circuit consists of a pair of conductors and the signal consists of a differential voltage between the two conductors. The voltage (with respect to ground) on one conductor of the pair will be mirrored or balanced by a voltage of equal magnitude but opposite polarity on the other conductor.

baseband data—The "normal" unmodulated form of a data signal as generated by digital circuitry. The term baseband is primarily used to emphasize the unmodulated nature of such a signal.

baseband LAN—A local area network which transfers data in baseband form only. This is in contrast to broadband LANs which handle modulated data signals.

baud—A unit for expressing the rate of symbol transfers. This term is often used synonymously with "bits per second," but such usage is incorrect. "Baud" refers to the number of symbols transferred in one second regardless of how many bits are represented by each symbol. For example, a Bell 212A modem operates at 600 baud, but since each symbol is a dibit, the data transfer rate is 1200 bits per second.

Baudot code—A term loosely used to refer to any of several similar five bit data codes commonly used in older teletype equipment. (See Tables 2-1 through 2-6.) Strictly speaking, this usage is in error since these codes are very different from the five bit codes developed by Baudot for the British Post Office telegraph system in 1874. (See Tables 2-7 and 2-8.)

Bell 103—A family of 300 bps FSK modem standards developed by the Bell System. These along with compatible models from other manufacturers have become virtually the only 300 bps modems in widespread use today.

Bell 201—A family of 2400 bps four-level DPSK modem standards developed by the Bell System. (See Fig. 9-2.)

Bell 202—A family of FSK modem standards developed by the Bell System. (See Fig. 9-3.) These modems operate at 1200 bps on dial-up lines, at 1400 bps on leased lines with C1 conditioning, and at 1800 bps on leased lines with C2 conditioning.

Bell 208—A family of 4800 bps eight-level PSK modem standards developed by the Bell System. (See Fig. 9-5.)

Bell 209A—A 9600 bps modem standard developed by the Bell System. This modem uses a combination of PSK and ASK called quadrature amplitude modulation. (See Fig. 9-6.)

Bell 212A—A 1200 bps four-level PSK modem standard developed by the Bell System. This modem can also operate in a 300 bps mode which is compatible with the Bell 103 standard.

bias distortion—A condition in which there is a significant difference between the nominally equal lengths of received marks and spaces. (See Fig. 3-19.)

Binary Synchronous Communications protocol—A character-oriented data-link protocol developed by IBM in the early 1960's which is still in widespread use today. The Bisync message format is shown in Fig. 11-2.

biphase coding—A line coding scheme in which a one is represented as a high-to-low signal transition occurring in the middle of the bit cell, while a zero is represented as a low-to-high transition. This is also referred to as Manchester II coding.

bipolar coding—Line coding schemes which involve both positive and negative voltages referenced to ground. This is in contrast to unipolar coding which uses either all positive or all negative voltages.

Bisync—See Binary Synchronous Communications protocol.

bit error rate—The average rate at which bit errors can be expected to occur in a particular system. This is usually expressed as a fraction in scientific notation—e.g. a BER of 2×10^{-6} means that an average of two bit errors can be expected for every million bits processed.

bit-oriented protocol—A type of data-link control protocol which does not use control characters. In fact, the data need not even be in character form—its nature is completely transparent to the data-link control protocol. Bit-oriented protocols are discussed in Chapter 12.

block check character—In general, any character appended to a message or transmission block for the purpose of error detection. In ANSI X3.28, the BCC is specifically defined as an even longitudinal parity check byte.

block parity—A error detection scheme in which both an LRC and VRC are used together to permit precise location of a single bit error within a block of data. (See Fig. 2-2.)

broadband LAN—A LAN in which use of the links is shared in a frequency-division fashion.

burst error—An error condition in which a number of contiguous or closely spaced bits all become corrupted.

bus topology—A LAN architecture in which the output drivers and input receivers of every node are connected directly to a lineal bus as shown in Fig. 13-14.

busy token—A unique bit pattern using token-passing access control schemes to indicate that a data packet or message immediately follows.

carrier-sense multiple access with collision detection—An access control scheme in which each station monitors the transmission medium for the presence of a carrier signal from another station. If none is detected, the station can then begin transmitting its message, while simultaneously monitoring the channel to insure that the message does not collide with messages from other stations which may have begun transmitting at approximately the same time. Upon detection of a collision, all transmitting stations cease transmission, wait for a random length time interval, and then—if the channel is available—retransmit the aborted message. By requiring each station to wait for a random time interval before attempting to retransmit, one station will usually begin before the other(s) and they will sense the busy channel and postpone their own retransmission attempts, thus minimizing the probability of repeated collisions.

catenate—To join two strings of text together end-to-end. Thus "AB" catenated with "DF" is "DFAB."

character-oriented protocols—Data-link control protocols which use special characters to frame the data characters and to control their exchange between communicating stations.

character parity—An error detection scheme in which an extra bit is added to each character. The value of the extra bit is set so that the total number of ONE bits in each character is either always even or always odd.

Cheapernet—A CSMA/CD local area networking system similar to Ethernet, but which uses cheaper cabling in exchange for a smaller maximum network size.

cipher text—The apparently random text which results from encrypting a message.

circuit switched routing—A communications technique in which a circuit connection between the communicating parties is established and maintained for the duration of the conversation or data exchange. Packet switching and message switching are alternative techniques.

closed system—A microcomputer system in which direct access to the system bus is not provided, and thus the owner/user is prevented from adding expansion cards and special interfaces to the basic computer. All peripherals must be connected through I/O ports provided by the manufacturer. The Apple Macintosh is an example of a closed system.

coaxial cable—Cable consisting of a central conductor surrounded by insulating material which in turn is surrounded by a hollow cylindrical conductive shield.

Comite' Consultatif Internationale de Telegraphique et Telephonique—A committee of the ITU concerned with standardization in data communications. The name of this committee is often Anglicized as "Consultative Committee in International Telegraphy and Telephony."

composite signal—The data signal on the trunk side of a multiplexer. This signal is a combination or composite of a number of individual user data signals which have been combined by the multiplexer.

concatenate—Synonymous with catenate.

conditioned line—A privately owned or leased telephone circuit which has been specially conditioned to improve its performance for data communications applications. Characteristics of various standard types of conditioning are shown in Figs. 5-14 through 5-25.

contention—The conflict which arises when two or more data sources simultaneously attempt to put data onto the same physical medium. At best, this will cause the loss of data if not detected; at worst it can cause damage to driver and receiver circuits if they are not designed to withstand the increased voltage or current levels which may be produced.

CRC-12—A twelve-bit cyclic redundancy checking scheme which uses $X^{12} + X^{11} + X^3 + X + 1$ as the generator polynomial. (See Fig. 2-3.)

CRC-16—A sixteen-bit cyclic redundancy checking scheme which uses $X^{16} + X^{15} + X^2 + 1$ as the generator polynomial. (See Fig. 2-3.)

CRC-CCITT—A sixteen-bit cyclic redundancy checking scheme which uses $X^{16} + X^{12} + X^5 + 1$ as the generator polynomial. (See Fig. 2-3.)

crosstalk—A condition in which signals on one communications circuit unintentionally appear on other nearby circuits due to inductive or capacitive coupling between the circuits.

cyclic redundancy checking—An error detection scheme which treats an N-bit message as an N-th order polynomial and divides it by a generator polynomial to produce a quotient and a remainder. This remainder is then appended to the message and transmitted. At the receiver, another remainder will be computed from the received data bits and compared to the received remainder. If errors have occurred during transmission, the two remainder values will not agree.

data access arrangement—A protective device required for connecting modems directly to telephone lines. DAA requirements are spelled out in FCC Rules, Part 68.

data circuit-terminating equipment—Terminology used in EIA RS-232-C and related documents to refer to modems or other equipment fulfilling a similar role. "Data communications equipment" is alternative terminology which has essentially the same meaning.

data code—A scheme for using various bit patterns to represent alphabetic, numeric, punctuation, and control characters. Data codes are discussed at length in Chapter 2.

data communications equipment—Terminology used in EIA RS-232-C and related documents to refer to modems or other equipment fulfilling a similar role. "Data circuit-terminating equipment" is alternative terminology which has essentially the same meaning.

data compression—A means for representing data in a more compact (i.e. fewer bits) form in order to save storage space or transmission time. Redundancies are removed, but no information is lost—after retrieval or reception of the compressed data it can be expanded exactly back into its original uncompressed form.

Data Encryption Standard—A standardized technique for encrypting data which has been endorsed by the National Bureau of Standards for use throughout the commercial world and non-defense areas of the government.

data-link control layer—The second layer of the ISO OSI model. This layer is concerned with establishment of an active link between stations, control of byte synchronization, datablock framing, error detection and correction, and regulation of the data flow rate over the link.

data terminal equipment—Terminology used in EIA RS-232-C and related documents to refer to terminals or other equipment fulfilling a similar role.

data transparency—An environment provided by the data-link control protocol in which any arbitrary sequence of data bits can be sent without interfering with normal link operation. Data transparency is required when the data to be transmitted may possibly contain bit sequences which could be interpreted as communications control characters. In character-oriented protocols, transparency can be provided by means of escape sequences or fixed length frame structures. (See Chapter 11.) In bit-oriented protocols, transparency is provided by zero-bit insertion deletion. (See Chapter 12.)

dataset—Bell System terminology which is synonymous with "modem."

decibel—A unit used for expressing relative amplitude or power.

delay distortion—Distortion of a signal caused by unequal delay of the different frequency components comprising the signal.

dibit—A data element which contains two bits.

differential phase-shift keying—A form of PSK in which the value of each bit or group of bits is contained in the relative phase shift from one symbol to the next rather than in the absolute phasing of the transmitted signal.

direct access adaptor—See data access arrangement.

double sideband signal—A signal which contains both the upper and lower sidebands produced by the "normal" modulation process. This is in contrast to single sideband or vestigial sideband in which one of the sidebands is either completely or partially removed. (See Figs. 6-3 through 6-5.)

dual tone multifrequency signaling—The generic name for the tone signaling method used on pushbutton or Touchtone® telephones. (See Table 5-2.)

echo suppression—A technique used by the telephone company to insure that a speaker will not have to listen to an echo of his own words returned by unavoidable coupling between the remote ends of the receive and transmit paths. A speech detector in the outbound path causes an attenuator to be switched into the inbound path whenever outbound speech is present.

Electronic Industries Association—An organization of companies involved in the electronics industry. EIA establishes standards such as RS-232-C, RS-449, etc. Information concerning EIA publications can be obtained from:
Electronic Industries Association
2001 Eye Street, N.W.
Washington, DC 20006

encryption—A means for securing data by transforming it into a seemingly random sequence of characters.

envelope delay—The amount of delay experienced by the various frequency components of a signal when traversing a communications channel. Envelope delay is also known as group delay.

Ethernet—A LAN standard developed by Xerox. Ethernet is discussed at length in Chapter 14.

extended binary-coded decimal interchange code—A data code, more commonly known as EBCDIC, which was developed by IBM. In new systems, ASCII has greatly supplanted the use of EBCDIC.

falltime—The time it takes for the falling edge of a pulse-type signal to fall from 90 percent of full scale to 10 percent of full scale.

FCC Rules Part 68—The section of FCC rules concerned with data access arrangements.

flooding—A routing scheme in tree topology LANs in which each intermediate node repeats each received message onto all of its outbound branch links.

Fourier series—A mathematical technique for computing the frequency spectrum of a periodic signal.

Fourier transform—A mathematical technique for computing the frequency spectrum of a timelimited aperiodic signal.

frequency division multiplexing—A multiplexing scheme in which a number of relatively narrowband low-capacity signals are modulated onto a number of carriers at different frequencies located within the passband of a relatively wideband composite channel. (See Fig. 10-7.)

frequency modulation—A form of modulation in which the frequency of the carrier is varied by an amount proportional to the instantaneous amplitude of the baseband signal.

frequency-shift keying—A form of frequency modulation in which the frequency of the carrier is modulated or keyed by a digital baseband signal.

full duplex circuit—A circuit which is capable of transmitting in both directions simultaneously.

fully connected mesh—A network topology in which every node has a direct connection to every other node. (See Fig. 13-1.)

generator polynomial—In CRC schemes, the polynomial which is divided into the message polynomial to produce the quotient and remainder.

group delay—See envelope delay.

half-duplex circuit—In North American usage, a half-duplex circuit is capable of transmitting in either direction, but only in a single direction at one time. As defined by the International Telecommunications Union, a half-duplex circuit is inherently capable of full-duplex operation but is restricted to transmitting in one direction at a time due to the limitations of the terminal equipment.

host—The main or central computer which supports a number of terminals communicating with it. In the case of a large mainframe with a number of remote terminals, the host-terminal relationship is clear and obvious. However, in the case of two personal computers connected via modems and a telephone circuit, it is not so obvious which computer is the host and which is the terminal. The distinction will actually depend upon the specific role which each takes in executing the communications protocol being used.

Huffman coding—A type of data coding scheme used to achieve some degree of data compression by using short code words to represent frequently used characters and longer code words to represent rarer ones. An example of a Huffman code is shown in Table 2-15.

IEEE 488—A standard for a general purpose interface bus which is frequently used as a local area network for digitally controlled laboratory instrumentation. (See Chapter 15.)

IEEE 802—A standard for several different types of local area network—CSMA/CD, token-bus, and token-ring.

in-band signaling—Telephone system signaling which is transmitted over the same path and within the same frequency band used for the voice signal.

interrupt—A mechanism by which elements of a computer system can request service from the central processor. Often this is more efficient than a polled approach in which the CPU must periodically interrogate each element to see whether or not it requires service.

intersymbol interference—The situation where adjacent and nearby symbols interfere with each other due to transmission at a rate too high for a given bandwidth.

ISO 3309—The international standard which defines the frame structure for the HDLC bit-oriented data-link control protocol.

ISO 4335—The international standard which defines the various procedural elements used in the HDLC bit-oriented data-link control protocol.

ISO 6159—The international standard which specifies which procedural elements are to be used in unbalanced operating configurations.

ISO 6256—The international standard which specifies which procedural elements are to be used in balanced operating configurations.

isochronous communications—Communications in which the transmitter and the distant receiver uses data clocks which have the same nominal rate, but which are not truly synchronous.

isochronous TDM—Time division multiplexing in which the individual user terminals each generate their own clock. These clocks are not mutually synchronized, but they are running at the same nominal rate. The isochronous multiplexers must provide some buffering and rate smoothing to compensate for the slight and unavoidable differences in the various user clock rates.

jitter—Variations in the width of received bits due to added noise which causes the received signal to cross the threshold between mark levels and space levels either slightly early or slightly late.

leased line service—Dedicated telephone circuits which can be leased from the telephone company on a monthly basis. Leased lines offer an advantage over the regular switched line service in that they can be specially selected and conditioned to optimize them for data transmission.

loading coil—Coils inserted by the telephone company into their longer local loops in order to introduce inductance to offset the distortion effects of line capacitance.

local loop—The circuit which runs from a subscriber site to the local telephone company office.

longitudinal parity—An error detection scheme in which an extra character is added to each block of data. The value of each bit in this character is set so that the total number of ONE bits in each bit position is either always even or always odd. (See Fig. 2-1.)

longitudinal redundancy check—Another name for longitudinal parity.

loopback—A test capability built into communications equipment such as multiplexers and modems. The transmit output is internally connected to the receive input, thus exercising all of the device circuitry, without requiring actual communication with a second similar device.

lowpass filter—A circuit which attenuates high frequency signals much more than the low frequency signals which pass through it.

Manchester coding—A line coding scheme in which a one is represented as a high-to-low signal transition occurring in the middle of the bit cell, while a zero is represented as a low-to-high transition. This is also referred to as biphase coding.

marking distortion—Bias distortion in which received marks appear longer than received spaces.

message switching—A scheme in which a complete data message is transmitted to a switching center where it is stored until the necessary links become available to forward the message to either its final destination or to the next switching center along the way.

modem—Devices used to modulate and demodulate digital data for transmission over various media not suited for baseband transmission.

modulation index—The ratio of the peak modulation amplitude to the peak carrier amplitude in an AM signal.

multiplexer—A device for combining a number of data signals into a single higher-bandwidth signal.

network layer—The portion of the ISO OSI model which is concerned with the routing of data from the source terminal to the destination terminal.

nonreturn to zero coding—A digital data signal format in which logical zeros are represented by nominally zero signal levels and logical ones are represented by some nonzero signal level.

on-off keying—A form of modulation which involves switching the carrier off and on in a pattern corresponding to the sequence of data bits.

open system—A microcomputer system which provides direct access to the system bus, permitting the owner/user to add expansion cards and special interfaces to the basic computer. The Apple II and IBM PC are examples of open systems.

out-band signaling—Telephone system signaling which is transmitted outside of the frequency band used for the voice signal.

packet switching—A switching technique in which the data traffic is broken up into short packets of approximately 100 to 2000 bits each. These packets are then sent using store-and-forward techniques.

phase modulation—A modulation technique in which the instantaneous phase deviation of the transmitted signal is made proportional to the modulating signal.

phase-shift keying—A form of phase modulation in which the modulating signal can take on only a few discrete values.

physical layer—The portion of the ISO OSI model which is concerned with defining the mechanical, electrical, functional, and procedural characteristics of the physical link between two communicating devices.

presentation layer—The portion of the ISO OSI model concerned with providing necessary services to interface a variety of applications to the communications system without requiring modifications to the applications software.

public key encryption—An encryption system which uses one key for encryption and a separate key for decryption. The encryption keys for a number of different users can be published in a public directory and used by anyone wishing to encrypt a message and send it to one of the listed users. Each user has a different decryption key which is kept private to insure that only the intended recipient can decrypt the message.

quadbit—A symbol which contains four bits of information.

recurrence coding—A data compression technique in which the sending system replaces strings of three or more identical characters with a special sequence consisting of a special character, a character count, and one of the original characters.

RG-58—A particular type of coaxial cable having a nominal characteristic impedance of 50 ohms.

RG-59—A particular type of coaxial cable having a nominal characteristic impedance of 75 ohms.

ring interface unit—A special device used in ring topology LANs for interfacing a terminal to the ring. By using high quality, well designed ring interface units, potentially unreliable terminals can be used without jeopardizing the entire network.

ringing—Oscillations which occur after a level transition in a digital signal. Ringing is usually caused by an impedance mismatch or an improperly terminated signal line.

risetime—The time it takes for the rising edge of a pulse-type signal to rise from 10 percent of full scale to 90 percent of full scale.

session layer—The portion of the ISO OSI model which is concerned with providing file management and bookkeeping functions needed to support intersystem communications.

simplex circuit—In North American usage, a simplex circuit can transmit in only one direction; but as defined by the ITU, a simplex circuit is capable of transmitting in either direction but only in a single direction at one time.

single sideband—A form of amplitude modulation in which one of the two sidebands is removed prior to transmission. (See Fig. 6-4.)

slotted ring—An access control scheme sometimes used in LANs with ring topologies. A number of tokens, separated by fixed-length slots for data packets continuously circulate around the ring. The fixed spacing between the tokens eliminates the need for complex token recognition hardware.

spacing distortion—Bias distortion in which received spaces appear longer than received marks.

star topology—A LAN topology in which links to all of the other stations radiate from a central hub station. (See Fig. 13-5.)

start bit—A bit sent at the beginning of each character in asynchronous transmission. Usually, an idle transmitter will send a continuous mark, and when it is ready to send a character it will begin with a start bit consisting of one space. (See Fig. 4-3.)

stop bit—A bit (or bits) marking the end of each character in asynchronous transmission. Usually, a transmitter will end each character by returning to a marking state. The stop bit is the interval (usually 1, 1.5, or 2 bit times) which the transmitter must remain in the marking state before it can begin the next character.

store-and-forward—A technique used in message switching, in which a message is transmitted to a switching center where it is stored until the necessary links become available to forward the message to either its final destination or to the next switching center along the way.

synchronous data transmission—Data transmission in which the transmitter and distant receiver are synchronized by operating off of the same bit clock, which is either sent in parallel with the data or embedded in and subsequently recovered from the data signal.

Synchronous Data Link Control—IBM's bit-oriented data-link protocol which is very similar to ISO HDLC.

synchronous TDM—Time division multiplexing in which the data clocks of the individual user signals are all derived from a master clock which is provided by the multiplexer.

switched network—When discussing telephone circuits, a term used to refer to the "regular" dialup network and distinguish it from the private and leased line services also used for data communications.

time division multiplexing—A scheme in which the individual bits in a number of user channels are spread apart and interleaved to form a single composite bit stream for long-haul transmission. (See Fig. 10-2.)

token passing—A popular access control technique used in LANs with ring topologies.

totem pole output—The output structure used in "regular" (i.e. not tri-state or open collector) TTL.

transport layer—The portion of the ISO OSI model which is concerned with the interface between the relatively hardware-oriented lower layers and the relatively software-oriented upper layers.

tribit—A data element which contains three bits.

unbalanced transmission—A method for transmission of baseband data in which each signal circuit consists of one signal conductor and a ground return.

V.21—A 200 bps full-duplex FSK modem recommendation by CCITT. (See Fig. 9-7.)

V.23—A CCITT modem recommendation for half-duplex FSK modems operating at either 600 bps or 1200 bps.

vertical redundancy check—Synonymous with character parity.

watchdog timer—A response timer used to insure that a station will not get hung up waiting for an expected response which never arrives.

X3.28—An ANSI standard containing a collection of character-oriented data-link control protocols for a variety of applications and system configurations.

XMODEM—A particular character-oriented protocol which is widely used in hobbyist-run computerized bulletin board systems.

zero-bit insertion/deletion—A technique used in bit-oriented protocols to break up runs of six or more contiguous ones to insure that they are not mistaken for flags or aborts.

Index

Other Bestsellers From TAB